BEHAVIORAL DECISION THEORY

George Wright is Senior Lecturer in Psychology and Director of the Decision Analysis Group at the City of London Polytechnic. He is also principal investigator on an Economic and Social Research Council project concerned with judgments of the likelihood of future events. He has taught the human aspects of decision-making to students of psychology, business studies, finance, and accountancy.

BEHAVIORAL DECISION THEORY

An Introduction

GEORGE WRIGHT

SAGE PUBLICATIONS
Beverly Hills   London   New Delhi

For my wife, Josephine

Copyright © 1984 by George Wright

All rights reserved. No part of this book may be reproduced or utilized in any form or by any means, electronic or mechanical, including photocopying, recording, or by any information storage and retrieval system, without permission in writing from the publisher.

For information address:

SAGE Publications, Inc.
275 South Beverly Drive
Beverly Hills, California 90212

SAGE Publications India Pvt. Ltd.　　　SAGE Publications Ltd
C-236 Defence Colony　　　28 Banner Street
New Delhi 110 024, India　　　London EC1Y 8QE, England

Printed in the United States of America

Library of Congress Cataloging in Publication Data

Wright, George, 1952-
  Behavioral decision theory.

  Bibliography: p.
  Includes index.
  1. Decision-making.　　I. Title.
BF441.W73　　1984　　　　　　153.8'3　　　　　　84-6889
ISBN 0-8039-2286-8

This U.S. edition published by arrangement with Penguin Books, Ltd, Harmondsworth, Middlesex, England. First published in the United Kingdom by Penguin in 1984.

FIRST PRINTING

Contents

Acknowledgements	8
Introduction	9
1 Subjective Expected Utility Theory as a Choice Principle	11
2 Estimation of Probability and Utility	29
3 Does Subjective Expected Utility Theory Describe Decision-making?	51
4 Individual and Cultural Differences in Decision-making under Uncertainty	67
5 Revision of Opinion	81
6 Descriptive Theories of Decision-making	97
Appendices	117
References	118
Index	127

Acknowledgements

This book is the product of about eight years' study of the psychology of decision-making. The book reflects my own background and own interests more than it does the complete field of decision-making.

My interest in decision-making started when I took my first job as a research assistant in the Decision Analysis Unit at Brunel University. There, as an apprentice to Larry Phillips and Patrick Humphreys, I learnt a great deal about conducting research in general and research on decision-making in particular. Research that the unit undertook consisted mainly of basic psychological research with an applied emphasis. I believe that these two influences show through in this book.

The next step in my own development was a job as research fellow in the Department of Behavioural Sciences at Huddersfield Polytechnic. Here I learnt the problems of teaching a fairly mathematical subject to non-mathematicians. This influence has led to a book that assumes no mathematical skills apart from addition, multiplication and long division. At Huddersfield the Dean of Education, David Legge, allowed me time and freedom to conduct my own research and make an initial start on this book. Under the leadership of John Maule this department has now gained approval for a multidisciplinary M.Sc. in the analysis of decision processes, the first in this country.

I now work as senior lecturer in the Department of Psychology at the City of London Polytechnic. Here, Larry Currie allowed me time to finish this book. I teach the psychology of decision-making to students of psychology, business studies, finance, and accountancy. This experience has led to a book which will, I believe, be of interest to students of all of these disciplines.

In management science, decision aids such as decision analysis are applied with little appreciation of their assumptions and psychological underpinning. This deficit is addressed in this book.

Introduction

What the Book Covers

This book is intended for psychologists, management scientists and, indeed, anyone interested in understanding the psychology of decision-making. The book assumes no background in complex mathematical skills but requires you to take part in several paper-and-pencil 'experiments' to give you an insight into the type of psychological research that has been undertaken. By the end of the book you will know, among other things, how good you are at dealing with uncertainty, how much value you place on money, whether decision analysis will improve *your* decision-making, and how good you are at revising your opinions as you gain more information.

The book is concerned with four major issues: How good are we at making decisions? Can decision-making be improved? How do we actually make decisions? and, Are some people better at making decisions than others?

What the Book Doesn't Cover

The book is concerned essentially with individual decision-making and makes no mention of decision-making in small groups or large organizations. Both of these topics are themselves large enough to be the subject of separate volumes. Similarly, the book does not delve deeply into the mathematical derivations of the normative decision theories of subjective expected utility and Bayes' theorem. However, the basic axiom systems underlying these theories are detailed in order to set the scene for a discussion of their psychological acceptability and, by extrapolation, the acceptability of their normative status.

1 Subjective Expected Utility Theory as a Choice Principle

Your Decision Problem

Imagine that you face the following decision problem.[1] One morning during half term you decide to spend the day either catching up on revision for an exam or taking a break from work by going for a picnic with a friend in the countryside. The weather, though, looks changeable. At present the sun is out but over the last few days it has rained. If the weather stays sunny and it does not rain you would rather go on the picnic with your friend. If it is going to rain then you would rather start your revision and leave the picnic until another day. If the weather is dull but at least it does not rain then you would rather be in the company of your friend, but you realize that your time could be usefully spent studying.

In the event that the sun shines but it also rains during the day you favour going for a picnic, for at least you will benefit from some sunshine.

Well, what would you do? Go on the picnic or stay indoors and study?

A difficult decision. Let us look at one way that it is possible to represent the problem, in the form of a payoff matrix. Figure 1a sets out the matrix for the two decisions or *acts* that are open to you, together with the four weather conditions that you consider possible. We shall call the possible weather conditions *events*, and we shall call the result of a particular event occurring when you have taken a particular action an *outcome*.

In Figure 1b I have replaced *your* verbal descriptions of the possible outcomes by some equally subjective numbers which we shall call *utilities*. Methods for the assessment of subjective value or utility will be discussed in detail in Chapter 2, for now we assume that the numbers are related directly to your verbal descriptions. A utility of 0 rep-

Behavioral Decision Theory

EVENTS

		Sunny, no rain	Overcast and rainy	Overcast	Sunny periods with some rain
ACTS	Go picnicking	Ideal picnic	Awful picnic	Mediocre picnic	Good picnic
	Study	Bad time to study	Best time to study	Poor time to study	Poor time to study

Figure 1a. Payoff matrix for your decision problem

EVENTS

		Sunny, no rain	Overcast and rainy	Overcast	Sunny rainy
ACTS	Go picnicking	100	0	50	75
	Study	10	90	40	40

Figure 1b. Numerical payoff matrix for your decision problem

resents the worst possible outcome: you go picnicking, but the sun does not shine and it rains. Conversely, a utility of 100 represents the best possible outcome: you go picnicking, the sun shines and it does not rain. The other possible outcomes fall between these two extremes in the same way that temperature varies between freezing point and boiling point on the centigrade scale. Of course, a dedicated student's utilities for the various outcomes may – differ from your own!

Well, what should you do? Go picnicking or stay at home and revise?

One way to make the decision would be to adopt a *maximax* strategy. Stated formally, you could be optimistic and choose the act that may maximize the maximum payoff. In our case this means go picnicking because there is a *possibility* of the sun shining but no rain, i.e. a utility of 100.

Subjective Expected Utility Theory as a Choice Principle

Another decision principle is the *maximin* strategy. This is a pessimistic choice principle in which you would choose the act that maximizes the minimum payoff. In our case this means you should stay at home and study because whatever happens to the weather you know that you will have a payoff of at least 10 *utilities*.

Well, would you decide by maximax or maximin? Perhaps you would not follow either of these principles. You may have noticed that neither maximax nor maximin makes any mention of the *probability* of the four weather conditions. Maximax is optimistic that the event resulting in the best outcome may happen, whereas maximin is pessimistic that the event resulting in the worst outcome may happen. But you will have some information about the probability of the four weather conditions. Recall that you know what the weather has been like over the last few days. Perhaps it has rained. This may lead you to think that it is now more likely to rain than not rain. However, the sun is presently shining and so there is some probability that the weather will be sunny. Perhaps you have heard the weather forecast for your part of the country and it indicated a cloudy day. Clearly, you may not be totally certain about which weather conditions will obtain *but* you are not so uncertain that it is worth deciding by maximax or maximin. In fact you may feel able to assess a probability or likelihood of each of the possible weather conditions occurring. Your probabilities will be *subjective* in that they are your own assessments and they may differ from the weather forecaster's assessments or, indeed, those of your friend.

Other probabilities may seem more *objective*. Imagine I have a coin in my hand which I am about to toss in the air. What is your estimate of the probability that it will land heads up? I think that everybody would agree that the probabilities of heads or tails are equal. However, assessment of equal probabilities is only an opinion and as such may be invalid. I happen to know the coin has two heads!

Therefore, probability shares a common property with utility in that subjective probabilities for the same event and utilities for the same outcome may vary from person to person. The question of who is the better probability-assessor and which is the best way to make probability assessments will be discussed in Chapter 2.

In our problem let us imagine that you consider that today the weather is fairly unlikely to be sunny with no rain, quite likely to be dull and rainy and highly unlikely to be solely dull. In addition, you consider there is a fair chance of sunny periods with some rain.

Behavioral Decision Theory

Now, I will substitute *numerical* probabilities for your *verbal* probability phrases. My substitutions are shown in Figure 2.

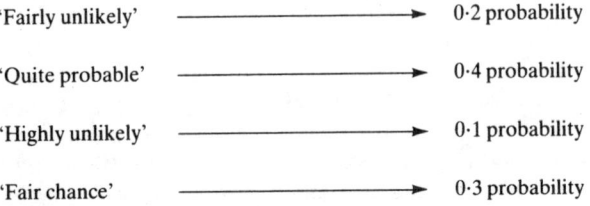

Figure 2. Substitution of numerical probabilities for your verbal probability phrases

For now we will assume that these numerical probabilities are a simple translation of your subjective states of uncertainty. I have allowed your probabilities to range from 0 to 1, with 0 meaning that you think it impossible that an event will occur and 1 meaning that you think it is absolutely certain that the event will occur. For example, a probability of 0·2 assigned to an event means that you believe that there are two chances out of ten, or a 20 per cent chance, of that event occurring.

Notice that the subjective probabilities attached to the four events which *you* consider possible sum to one. This is because you believe that *one* of the four weather conditions *must* occur. Consider a single throw of a dice which has six sides. The probability of a *named* single side, say a 4, landing face up is one sixth. The probability of *any* one side landing face up is 1, i.e. certainty. More formally, the probabilities of a set of mutually exclusive and exhaustive events *must* sum to one. In your half-term holiday decision problem, you may believe that other weather events are possible. If you do, then it follows that your probabilities given to the four events need not sum to 1; you may have some probability to distribute to other weather events.

However, for simplicity's sake we will restrict our analysis to the four possible weather states we discussed earlier in the chapter.

You now have two types of information on which to base your decision, utility and subjective probability. How should you combine this information?

Subjective Expected Utility Theory (SEU)[2] specifies one method of combination. Here, the 'Subjective Expected' refers to *your* prob-

Subjective Expected Utility Theory as a Choice Principle

abilities and 'Utility' refers to *your* utilities. The SEU for a *particular* act is made up of the total of the products of probability and utility for each combination of act and event. In our case the SEU for picnicking is $(0·2 \times 100) + (0·4 \times 0) + (0·1 \times 50) + (0·3 \times 75) = 47·5$. The SEU for studying is $(0·2 \times 10) + (0·4 \times 90) + (0·1 \times 40) + (0·3 \times 40) = 54$.

The next step is to choose the act which *maximizes* SEU. In this case you should stay at home and study, for this is worth a subjective expected utility of 54, whereas going picnicking is worth only 47·5.

In this instance maximin and 'maximization of SEU' (which I shall now abbreviate to SEU) specify the same decision: stay at home and study; but it is easy to see that, if your subjective probabilities were to change, the two choice principles may specify different acts. Which choice principle should you follow? Should you disregard both and follow your intuition?

I will now present an argument that SEU is the better choice principle and that your decision should follow SEU even if the prescriptions of SEU and your intuitive feelings conflict. SEU can be shown to be a *normative* theory of decision-making under uncertainty that specifies how decisions *should* be made.

SEU as a Normative Theory

SEU is a theory of decision that is derived from certain axioms or fundamental principles. *If* you accept the axioms then it follows, in an analogous way to the proof of Pythagoras' theorem, that SEU is the *rational* or *normative* theory of decision-making for you. In other words you should follow the decisions prescribed by SEU even if your intuitive decision contradicts the decision prescribed by SEU.

There are four basic axioms of SEU:[3] decidability, transitivity, dominance and the sure-thing principle.

1. Decidability

This axiom states that if you have to evaluate two possible outcomes, A and B, then you should be able to say whether you prefer outcome A to outcome B or vice versa, or whether you are equally indifferent to the two outcomes. For example, try to evaluate your preferences between the two outcomes, ideal picnic and awful picnic.

Behavioral Decision Theory

2. Transitivity

If you prefer outcome A to outcome B and you also prefer outcome B to outcome C, you should prefer outcome A to outcome C. For example, if you prefer an ideal picnic to a mediocre picnic and also prefer a mediocre picnic to an awful picnic you should prefer an ideal picnic to an awful picnic.

3. Dominance

If for every possible event, act 1 produces at least as desirable an outcome as act 2 and if, for at least one event, the outcome of act 1 is better than that of act 2, you should prefer act 1 to act 2. Figure 3 sets out an example of dominance in the form of the now familiar payoff matrix. Here act 1 dominates act 2.

	Event 1	Event 2	Event 3
Act 1	100	50	70
Act 2	90	50	70

Figure 3. Dominance in a payoff matrix

4. Sure-Thing Principle

When you are in the process of making a choice between possible acts, the outcomes that are not related to your choice should not influence your choice. Figure 4 sets out an example of the sure-thing principle.[4] Matrix 1 should be seen as an equivalent decision problem to matrix 2, because the occurrence of a market crash produces the same outcome whichever act is chosen. In other words, the possibility of the market crash should not influence your decision as to which shares to buy.

If you accept these four axioms, in combination with some others that are of minor importance, then three consequences follow. These are: (1) that probabilities exist on a ratio scale (extending from 0 to 1); (2) that utilities exist on an interval scale (extending between two arbitrary points, say 0 to 100 with the property that a score of, say, 50 has twice as much utility as a score of 25); (3) that maximization of subjective expected utility is your optimal choice criterion.

Subjective Expected Utility Theory as a Choice Principle

Matrix 1

		EVENTS		
		Economy worsens	Economy improves	Market crash
ACTS	Buy stable industries' shares	Small loss (about £100)	Small gain (about £50)	Lose £500
	Buy Speculation Incorporated's shares	Large loss (about £400)	Large gain (about £500)	Lose £500

Matrix 2

		EVENTS	
		Economy worsens	Economy improves
ACTS	Buy stable industries' shares	Small loss (about £100)	Small gain (about £50)
	Buy Speculation Incorporated's shares	Large loss (about £400)	Large gain (about £500)

Figure 4. Payoff matrices illustrating the sure-thing principle for share purchase

But the crucial question is: do you accept the axioms? In the above section I introduced the axioms in a relatively uncontroversial way so that I think it is almost certain that they were accepted as reasonable. Other researchers have not been so uncritical; they have presented the axioms, most notably the sure-thing principle, in the form of 'paradoxes'. This research will be discussed in detail in Chapter 3; for the moment we will conclude, tentatively, that SEU has normative status. In other words, if your intuitive decisions tend to conflict with SEU prescribed decisions it follows that if, in the future, you choose the acts that have the highest subjective expected utilities, your decision-making will become improved.

Given the evidence discussed so far, this conclusion is, I believe, fairly uncontroversial and appealing. Indeed, in the 1960s the technology of SEU, *decision analysis*, was evolved by pioneers like Howard Raiffa and Robert Schlaifer to improve decision-making. Decision

Behavioral Decision Theory

analysis is now widely used as an aid to business and government decision-making, especially in the United States where it was initially developed.

Consider Figure 5, which is a decision analytic representation of a real-life decision problem which I have adapted from Christensen-Szalanski and Bushyhead (1979).[5] The *decision tree* representation of

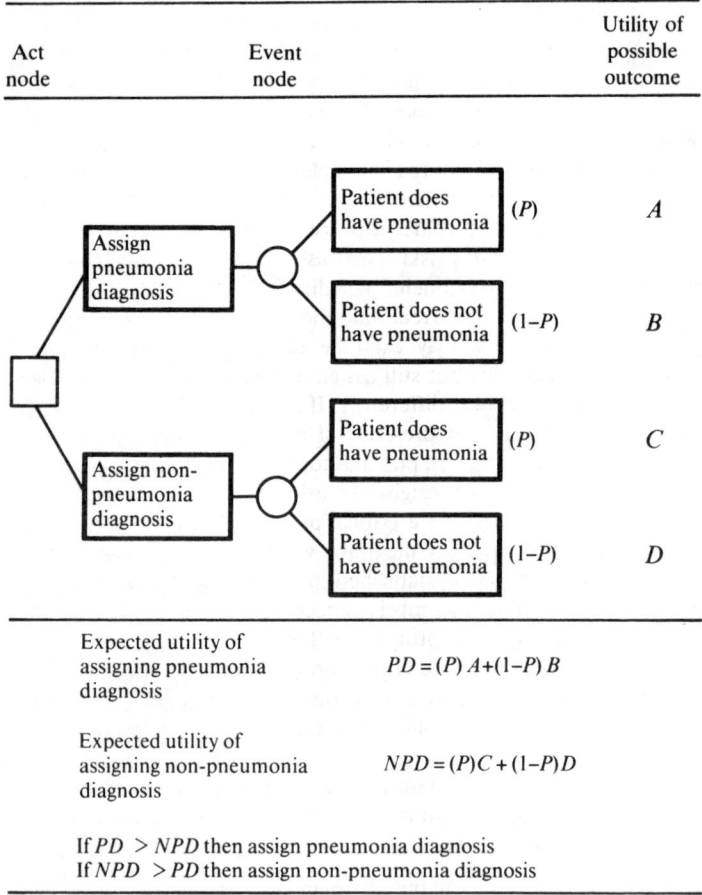

Figure 5. Decision analysis applied to a pneumonia diagnosis problem

Subjective Expected Utility Theory as a Choice Principle

the problems flows from left to right to represent the temporal sequence of acts and events. Conventionally, a square is taken to represent an act choice, and a circle, two or more events that could occur at one point in time. This particular decision analysis represents a physician's decision of whether to assign a pneumonia diagnosis or assign a non-pneumonia diagnosis. For each course of action there are two possible outcomes: the patient does have pneumonia, or the patient does not have pneumonia.

The physician is first required to estimate the subjective probability that the patient has pneumonia (P). Given this subjective probability estimate and the physician's utility for the possible consequences of the decision (A to D) it is then possible to calculate the expected utility for each diagnostic assignment. The act, or in this case the diagnosis, with the highest expected utility is then chosen in a similar manner to the picnic/study decision problem.

Both probabilities and utilities are crucial in determining the decision. As Christensen-Szalanski and Bushyhead note, the physician could appropriately assign a pneumonia diagnosis even when he or she believes it less likely to be correct than the non-pneumonia diagnosis. Similarly, two physicians may estimate the same probability of a patient having pneumonia but still assign different diagnoses because they value the consequences differently. If a physician is making many diagnoses of the absence or presence of a specific disease or illness where the set of utilities for the possible consequences of the diagnoses remain unchanged, it is a straightforward extension of the decision analytic approach to calculate a critical probability for diagnosis. At the critical probability neither diagnosis would be favoured. After a critical probability has been established, precise specification of probability of illness for future patients is unnecessary; all the physician has to do is to assess whether the probability that a given patient has pneumonia falls above or below the critical probability.

The pneumonia example is a very simple application of decision analysis using the principle of subjective expected utility maximization as a choice criterion.

Next I will present another 'real-life' decision problem which I would like you to attempt to represent in terms of a decision tree. Use a clean sheet of paper.

> Imagine that you are a businessman and you are considering making electronic calculators.

Your factory can be equipped to manufacture them and you recognize that other companies have made a lot of money from producing them. However, equipping the factory for production will cost quite a lot of money and you have seen the price of calculators dropping steadily. What should you do?

Well, what's the correct decision analytic representation? Figure 6 presents one representation which may, or may not, match yours.

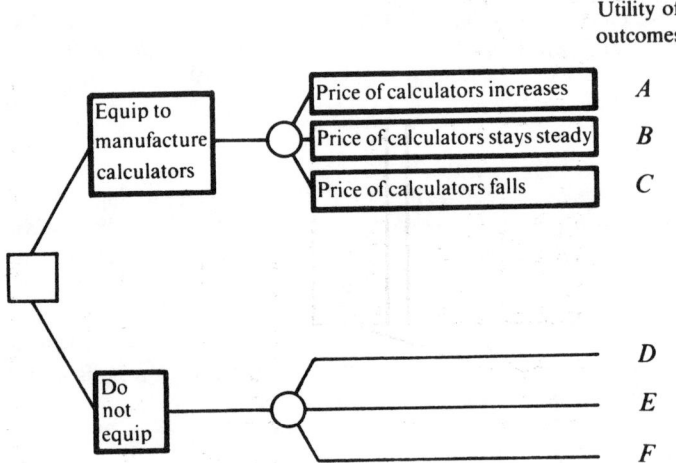

Figure 6. One decision analytic representation of the calculator problem

Figure 7 is a more elaborate and perhaps more realistic representation of the problem.

Do you agree? Actually, as you've probably guessed, there is no *obviously* right or wrong representation of any problem that is in any way related to real life. Although SEU may be an optimal decision principle there is no normative technique for *eliciting* the structure of the decision problem from the decision-maker. It's really a matter of the decision analyst's judgement as to whether the elicited tree is a fair representation of the decision-maker's decision problem. Once a structure is agreed then the computation of SEU is fairly straightforward. The major problem in decision analysis is the structuring of the decision problem, for if the structuring is wrong then it is a necessary

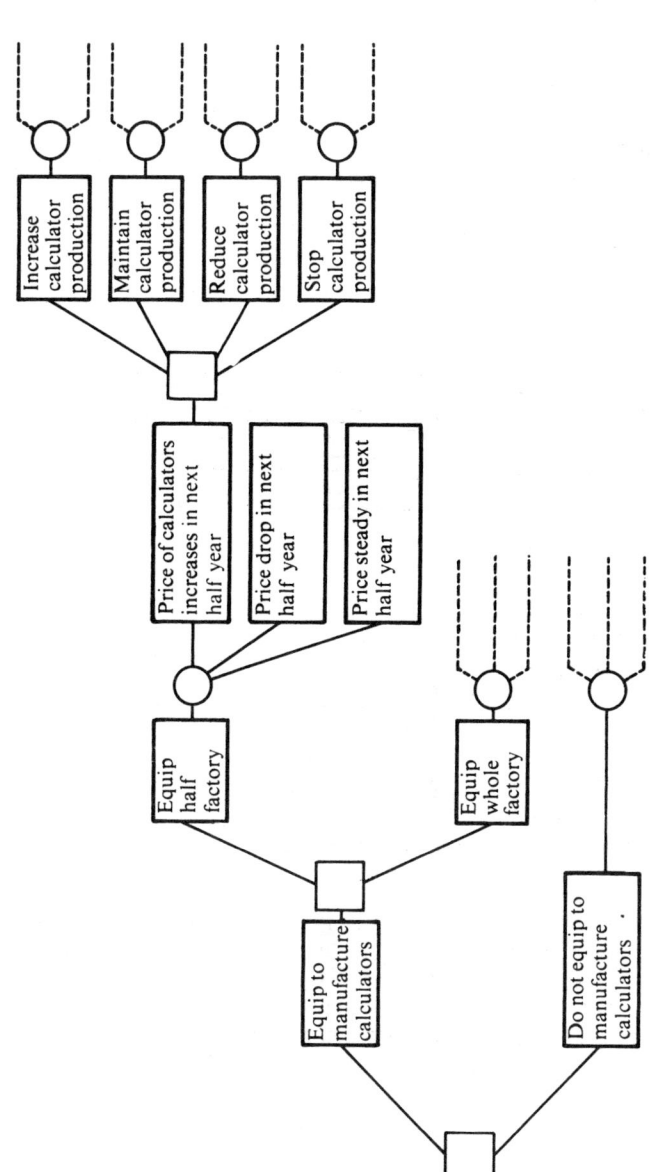

Figure 7. Towards the correct decision analytic representation of the calculator problem?

Behavioral Decision Theory

consequence that subsequent assessments of utilities and probabilities may be inappropriate and the SEU computations may be invalid. Almost no research exists on whether analytic structures such as

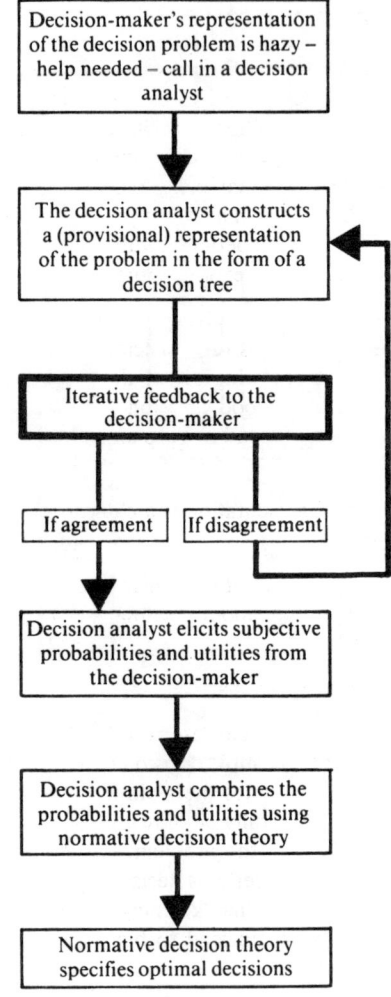

Figure 8. Phases of a decision analysis

Subjective Expected Utility Theory as a Choice Principle

decision trees adequately model the decision-maker's internal representation of a decision problem in a reliable and valid way.

Figure 8 presents a description of the phases in a decision analysis of a decision problem that the decision-maker wishes to resolve with the help of the practitioner of decision analysis – the decision analyst.

Stages 2 and 3 of the decision process are iterative, the structure of the decision problem emerges from discussions between the decision-maker and the analyst. Once a structure for the decision representation has been agreed and probabilities and utilities are elicited (stage 4) the SEU for the various acts under consideration can be computed (stage 5) and the act which has the maximal SEU is chosen (stage 6).

What determines the decision analyst's provisional representation of the decision problem? Past experience with similar classes of decision problems and, to a significant extent, intuition.

To quote von Winterfeldt:

> 'Often the analyst decides on a specific structure and later finds it unmanageable . . . knowing about the recursive nature of the structuring process, it is good decision analysis practice to spend much effort on structuring and to keep an open mind about possible revisions' (p. 74).[6]

However, problem representation is a clinical art rather than a science, as Fischhoff notes:

> 'Regarding the validation of particular assessment techniques, we know . . . next to nothing about eliciting the structure of problems from decision-makers.'[7]

Keeney has fewer reservations:

> 'Often the complex problems are so involved that their structure is not well understood. A simple decision tree emphasizing the problem structure which illustrates the main alternatives, uncertainties, and consequences, can usually be drawn up in a day. Not only does this often help in defining the problem, but it promotes client and colleague confidence that perhaps decision analysis can help. It has often been my experience that sketching out a simple decision tree with a client in an hour can lead to big advances in the eventual solution to a problem.'[8]

Several computer aids have been developed to aid decision-makers place a structure on a decision problem. These aids are not concerned so much with the content or substance of the decision problem as with its analytic structure. One program, OPINT (Kelly, 1978), focuses on the acts available to the decision-maker, the possible events and their temporal sequencing. It helps formulate decision tree representation. Another computer program, MAUD (Humphreys and Wisudha[9]), aids elicitation of the subjective valuation, or utility, of the outcomes or goals under consideration.

However, as von Winterfeldt[10] points out, such analytic aids may have a wide range of flexible applicability over substantive problem areas, but they concentrate on fundamentally empty structures and must consider each decision problem from scratch. Also, these decision analytic structures, deriving as they do from decision theory, may bear no correspondence to real-world problems. By contrast, von Winterfeldt advocates the development of what he calls 'prototypical decision analytic structures' which have more substance than decision trees or goal trees. He identifies general classes of problems with common features. One set of such problems is environmental standard setting and regulation, which encompasses noise pollution, oil discharge standards, and emission standard setting. These decisions have the common features of involving a regulatory agency (usually the client of the decision analyst), an industrial concern or developer, and impactees (usually the affected public). A common game theoretic structure can be shown to be prototypical to standard setting in all these areas. Similarly, contingency decisions where plans are made for possible disasters can be analysed using prototypical structures. Military offensives, decisions involving gas plant explosions and oil platform blow-outs all have the common characteristics of: numerous decisions having to be made simultaneously; information coming in rapidly; and potentially unexpected events occurring. In essence, von Winterfeldt advocates the development of problem-driven, but still generalizable structures and models:

> 'Prototypical decision analytic structures . . . are developed to meet the substantive characteristics of a given problem, but are at the same time general enough to apply to similar problems . . .'
>
> 'Today decision analysis books have chapters such as simple decisions under uncertainty and multi-attributed evaluation problems. I am looking forward to chapters such as "siting industrial facilities; pollution control management" and "contingency planning".'

Subjective Expected Utility Theory as a Choice Principle

By contrast, the next section of this chapter strikes a note of caution by outlining research suggesting that the initial representation of a decision problem, whether in the guise of a formal prototype or as a result of the decision analyst's intuition and past experience, may have a significant negative effect on the decision-maker's understanding of the problem under consideration.

Inherent Problems of Decision Representation: 'Out of Sight, Out of Mind'

Many decision-makers report that they feel the process of problem representation is perhaps more important than the subsequent SEU computations. Humphreys has labelled the latter the 'direct value' of decision analysis and the former the 'indirect value'. Decision analysis provides the decision-maker with a

> 'convincing rationale for choice, improves communication and permits direct and separate comparisons of different people's conceptions of the structure of the problem, and of the assessment of decomposed elements within their structures, thereby *raising consciousness* about the root of any conflict'.[11]

However, some studies have illustrated that the decision-makers' estimates, judgement and choices are affected by the way knowledge is elicited. This research has direct relevance for the decision analysts' attempts at structuring. In one study, Fischhoff, Slovic and Lichtenstein[12] investigated estimation of failure probabilities in decision problem representations called fault trees. These fault trees are essentially similar to decision trees with the exception that events rather than acts and events are represented. Figure 9 gives a fault tree representation for the event 'a car fails to start'. This is the full version of the fault tree that Fischhoff *et al.* produced from the use of several car repair reference texts.

In several experiments Fischhoff *et al.* presented various 'full' and 'pruned' fault trees to members of the public. For example, three of the first six sub-events in Figure 9 would be omitted from the presentation to be implicitly included under the seventh sub-event 'all other problems'. The subjects of Fischhoff *et al.* were asked:

> 'For every 100 times that a trip is delayed due to a "starting failure" estimate, on average, how many of the delays are caused by the 7(4) factors?'

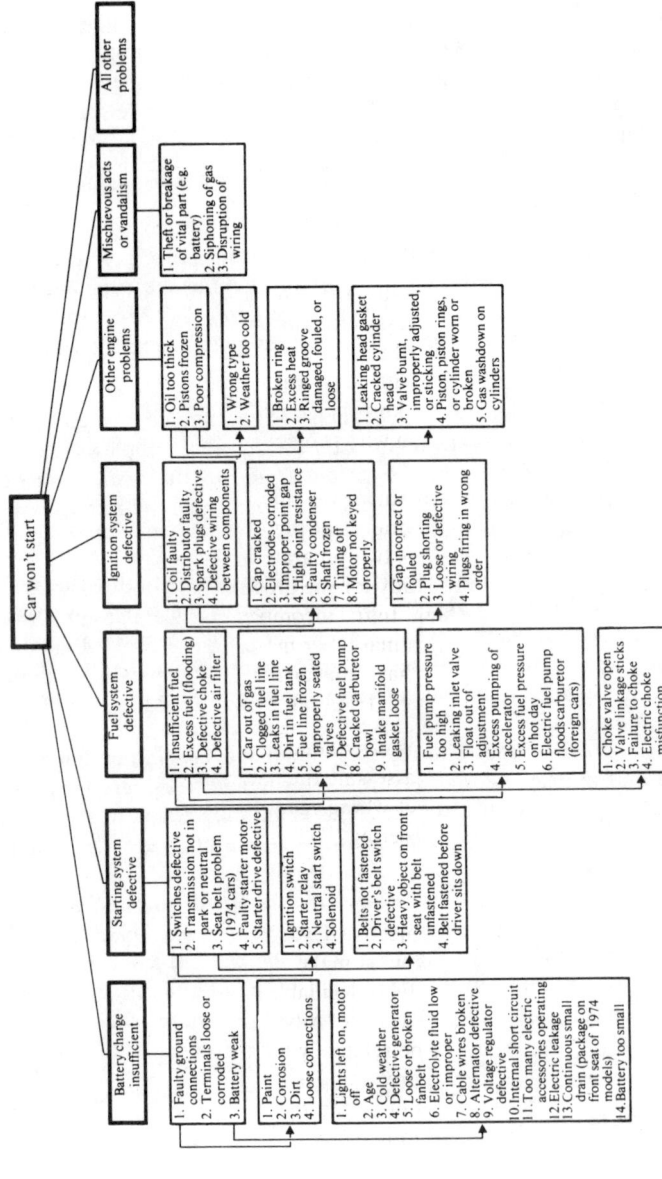

Figure 9. A possible fault tree for discovering why a car won't start
From B. Fischhoff, P. Slovic and S. Lichtenstein, 'Fault trees: Sensitivity of estimated failure probabilities to problem representation' (see note 12). Copyright © The American Psychological Association, 1978. Adapted by permission of the authors

Subjective Expected Utility Theory as a Choice Principle

Fischhoff *et al.* found that the amount of probability placed on 'all other problems' did not increase significantly when it contained three of the other main sub-events. In a subsequent experiment the importance of 'all other problems' was emphasized by Fischhoff, by asking subjects:

> 'In particular we would like you to consider its [the fault tree's] completeness. That is, what proportion of the possible reasons for a car not starting are left out, to be included in the category, "all other problems"?'

However, focusing subjects' attention on what was missing only partially improved their awareness. Fischhoff *et al.* labelled this insensitivity to the incompleteness of the fault tree 'out of sight out of mind'. The finding was confirmed with technical experts, garage mechanics. Neither self-rated degree of knowledge nor actual garage experience had any significant association with subjects' ability to detect what was missing from the fault tree.

Another finding from the study was that the perceived importance of a particular sub-event or branch of the fault tree was increased by presenting it in pieces (i.e. as two separate branches).

The implications of this study for the growing field of decision analysis are, I think, far-reaching. Initial incomplete problem presentations presented as informal 'bench marks' or more formal 'prototypes' may lead the decision-maker to have unwarranted overconfidence in the stated problem representation. To quote Fischhoff:

> '. . . Decision Analysis is orientated to picking the apparent best alternative rather than to assessing the adequacy of our knowledge, it may encourage us to act where ignorance dictates hesitation or continued information gathering.'[13]

Summary

This chapter introduced Subjective Expected Utility Theory (SEU) as a normative theory of how to make decisions under uncertainty. The four basic axioms of SEU, decidability, transitivity, dominance and the sure-thing principle, were described and, in the form they were introduced, were shown to be relatively uncontroversial. Inputs to an SEU analysis of subjective probabilities for the occurrence of events, and subjective values or utilities for the outcomes of events, were shown to vary from person to person.

Behavioral Decision Theory

Finally, decision analysis, the technology of SEU, was introduced and an example was given of its use in a clinical setting. Problems of structuring a decision problem, before application of SEU, were described.

2 Estimation of Probability and Utility

The previous chapter described the use of subjective expected utility maximization as a choice principle using inputs of subjective probability and utility. We will now review methods for the elicitation of these probabilities and utilities. As we saw earlier, subjective probabilities for the occurrence of an event and utilities for the consequences of that event vary from person to person. It follows that probability and utility assessment may be subject to external and internal influences. The second part of this chapter outlines some of the contexts that influence and, in some cases, bias assessments. Finally, a method is introduced that allows evaluation of the realism of assessed probabilities.

Measuring Probability

As we saw in Chapter 1, if you, as the decision-maker, accept the axioms of SEU then it follows logically that probabilities exist and are measured on a ratio scale extending from 0 to 1. These probabilities or degrees of belief combine according to the laws of probability. However, there are several different methods for the elicitation of these probabilities and, as we shall see, sometimes these methods do not produce an identical probability assessment for the same event.[1]

The *direct method* for probability assessment is very simple; you are simply required to state a number between 0 and 1, with 0 meaning you think that it is impossible that an event will occur and 1 meaning you think it is absolutely certain that the event will occur. Answer the next question yourself.

What is your probability that it will be raining on the roof of your home at precisely 11 a.m. tomorrow morning?_____

Behavioral Decision Theory

Let's vary the response mode slightly. Give your answer to the above question in odds. Odds of 1 to 1 would mean that you think that the event's occurrence is equally likely as its non-occurrence. Odds of 1,000 to 1 *against* would mean that you think the event's occurrence was extremely unlikely. Conversely, odds of 1,000 to 1 *on* would mean you think that the event's occurrence is extremely likely. Put your answer here: _____ to _____.

Now add together the two numbers and divide the number on the left by this sum. This will convert your odds response to probability. For example, odds of 10 to 1 against the event happening is equivalent to a probability of 0·91 that the event will not happen or 0·19 that the event will happen. Odds of 10 to 1 on are equivalent to a 0·91 probability that the event will happen. You may have found that your converted odds response is not identical to your direct probability estimate. Don't worry – we'll return to this issue later.

Next we will consider an indirect way of measuring your degree of belief. Consider wager A presented in Figure 1. If it does rain at 11 a.m. tomorrow over your home you win £100; if it doesn't you win nothing.

Now consider wager B, which refers to the 'spinner bet' consisting of a pointer which is free to rotate over a circle comprising two colours, black and white. I can adjust the relative amount of these two colours. If the pointer lands in the black you win £100; if it lands in the white you win nothing. Given that the proportion of black and white sectors is that in Figure 1, which wager would you prefer, wager A or wager B? or are you indifferent between the wagers?

If you preferred wager A to wager B then I would increase the proportion of black to white until you prefer wager B to wager A. I would then reduce the proportion of black until you are indifferent between the two wagers. The relative proportion of black to white would then be equivalent to your subjective probability that it will rain tomorrow. This indifference bet method allows *me* to measure your subjective probability without requiring *you* to state any numbers to describe your degree of belief. The only restriction in this method is that the utilities of the outcomes in the two wagers must be strictly identical. In this instance wager B must be played at, or shortly after, 11 a.m. tomorrow, when we know whether it has actually rained or not. If the result of wager B was to be paid out now, your utility for an 'instant' £100 may be higher than that for a 'delayed' £100 and so the two wagers would not be strictly identical.

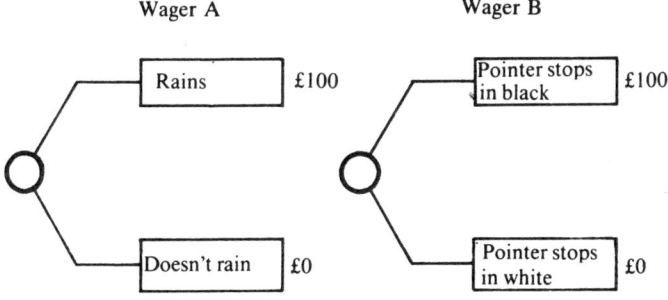

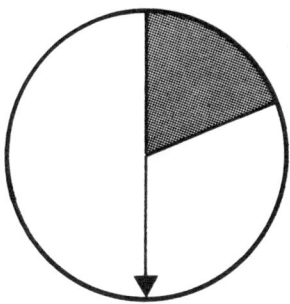

Figure 1. Indirect measurement of probability

Notice that although people may differ in their utility for £100, this amount is similar in both wagers and therefore has no bearing on the measurement of subjective probability.

Which of these three methods is the best for elicitation of subjective probability? The empirical evidence is, unfortunately, contradictory. Sometimes the indirect methods are inconsistent with direct methods and sometimes they are not. Some studies have shown consistency between probability estimates inferred from wagers and direct estimates.[2] However, other studies have shown that statistically naive subjects were inconsistent between direct and indirect assessment methods, whereas statisticians were not.[3] Generally, direct odds estimates, perhaps because they have no upper or lower limit, tend to be more extreme than direct probability estimates.

Behavioral Decision Theory

If probability estimates derived by different methods for the same event are inconsistent, which method should be taken as the true index of degree of belief?

One way to answer this question is to use the method of assessing subjective probability that is most reliable. In other words there should be high agreement between the subjective probabilities, assessed at different times by a single assessor for the same event, given that the assessor's knowledge of the event is unchanged. Unfortunately, there has been relatively little research on this important problem. Goodman reviewed the results of several studies using direct estimation methods. Test–retest correlations were all above 0·88 with the exception of one study using students assessing odds – here the reliability was 0.66. Goodman concluded that most of the subjects in all experiments were very reliable.[4]

Whatever direct or indirect method of obtaining a numerical estimate is used it is clear that the elicited probabilities can be utilized easily in a SEU analysis. By contrast, consider verbal reports of uncertainty, for example, 'very probable' or 'extremely likely'. These estimates are less precise than numerical estimates and interpretation of their meaning varies from person to person. Table 1 sets out the variation in numerical meaning attributed to some probability expressions found by Lichtenstein and Newman.[5] Also notice the asymmetry found between mirror-image pairs. Clearly verbal expressions of probability are open to misinterpretation.

Table 1. Variations in the numerical meaning of probability expressions

	Mean associated probability	Range of associated probabilities
Highly probable	0·89	0·60–0·99
Quite likely	0·79	0·30–0·99
Probable	0·71	0·01–0·99
Possible	0·37	0·01–0·99
Improbable	0·12	0·01–0·40
Quite unlikely	0·11	0·01–0·50
Highly improbable	0·06	0·01–0·30

Estimation of Probability and Utility

Measuring Utility

Utility is subjective value and subjective values by definition vary from person to person. A millionaire would, perhaps, place less value on a 50p piece than you; he probably wouldn't bend down to pick it up from the street if he dropped it. Utility, as we noted in Chapter 1, is measured on an interval scale so it follows that the zero point and unit of measurement are arbitrary. Utility is, therefore, relative.

We are now going to measure your own utility for money, up to a limit of £10,000, by means of a lottery question. Please answer all parts of the question.

LOTTERY QUESTION

Here is a special lottery ticket:

> 50% chance to win £10,000
> 50% chance to win £0

The holder of the ticket is entitled to play the game written on the ticket. The game in this case is a fair event – a coin toss giving a 50 per cent chance of winning nothing. *The holder of the ticket can only play the game once* and so might win £10,000 or nothing.

Imagine that you have been given the ticket as a gift. Therefore you are entitled to play the game any time this week. Obviously this ticket has some value to you and you consider selling it. Imagine a friend has volunteered to sell it for you for no charge. Your friend will ask people how much they are willing to give for it and sell to the highest bidder.

What is the lowest amount you would accept for the ticket? In other words, if nobody offers more than this amount you would rather keep the ticket and play the game.

Put the amount in the triangle here:

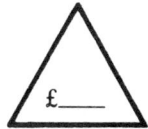

Behavioral Decision Theory

Ticket 2

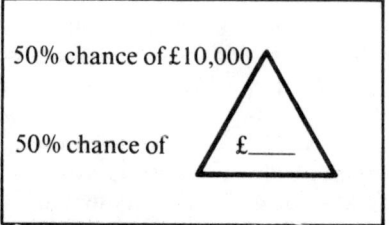

Insert the amount you put in the previous triangle here.

Now, try to forget that you ever assessed the first ticket and imagine that you own only ticket 2. What is the lowest amount that you would accept for this ticket? (Remember you can only play the game once.)
Put the amount here:

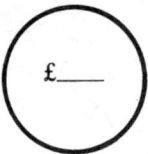

Ticket 3

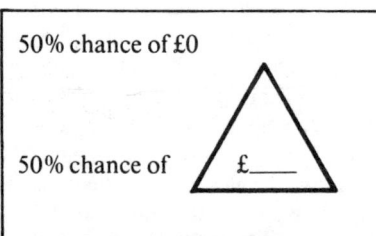

Insert the amount you put in the previous triangle here.

Now, try to forget that you ever owned the second ticket and imagine that you own only ticket 3. What is the lowest amount that you would accept for this ticket? (Remember you can only play the game once.)
Put that amount here:

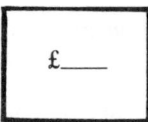

Estimation of Probability and Utility

Plot the amount you placed in the triangle opposite the 50 utile mark (utiles are units of utility) on the vertical axis in Figure 2. By using monetary expectation this amount should be £5,000 (i.e. 0·5 × £10,000 + 0·5 × £0). You may find your amount is less than £5,000. Next, plot the amount you placed in the circle opposite the 75 utile mark and, finally, plot the amount you placed in the square next to the 25 utile mark.

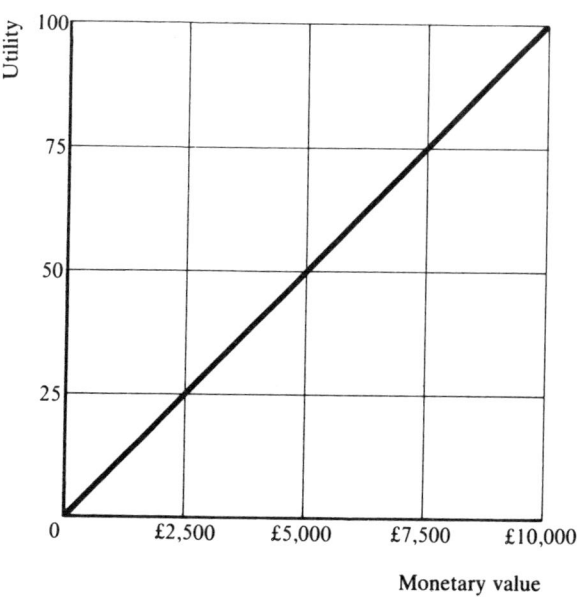

Figure 2. Your utility for money

This method for measuring utility makes the assumption that the desirability of an event does not influence its probability, that is, more attractive consequences are not seen as more likely or, alternatively, more likely consequences are not seen as more attractive. We will return to this issue later, in Chapter 3; for the moment we assume that this assumption is satisfied.

What did your utility function for money look like? Figure 3 presents three exemplar utility functions. Most people show a utility function that resembles the 'risk-averse' curve, a little money has a very high utility whereas large amounts of money have roughly the same utility.

Behavioral Decision Theory

Clearly there would be serious implications for decision analysis if monetary value were used in SEU computations instead of utility for money. A 'risk-seeking' curve would characterize someone for whom small to moderate amounts of money have roughly the same low utility.

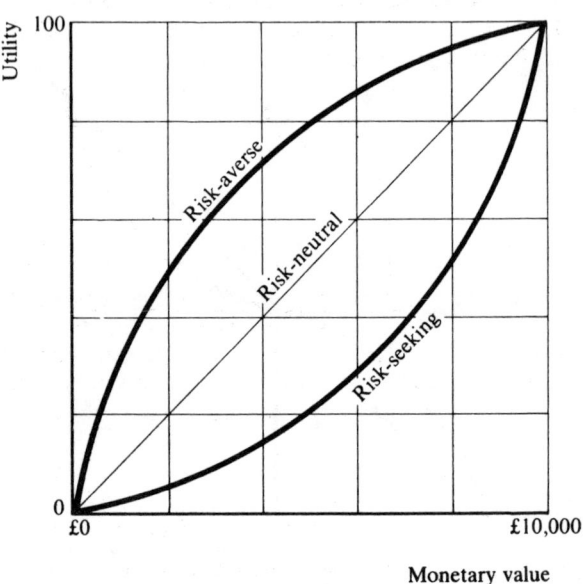

Figure 3. Three exemplar utility functions

As we arbitrarily fixed the utility of £0 at zero and £10,000 at 100, the utility of £10,000 for the people characterized in Figure 3 is identical. Clearly, if we had assigned a utility of 100 to £100,000 the three types of people would show different utilities for £10,000. In other words, utility assessment is influenced by the assessment procedure. What would happen to the shape of your utility function for money if you were suddenly given a gift of £5,000? Would your utility for small to moderate amounts of money lessen? Markowitz suggested that an individual's utility function for money is constant and that the shape of the utility curve is relative to the *current wealth* of the individual. In other words the curve measures the utility for *n* more pounds.[6]

Estimation of Probability and Utility

Common sense tells us that individuals cannot be classified simply as 'risk-seekers' or 'risk-avoiders'. Most of us take out insurance to protect ourselves from large losses and at the same time most of us gamble either on fruit machines, lotteries or horses. If an individual both insures and gambles, what would be the shape of his or her utility curve? Figure 4 describes this behaviour in terms of utility for money. However, as we will see later in this chapter and also in Chapter 3, biases in probability estimation may be another explanation of gambling and insurance purchase.

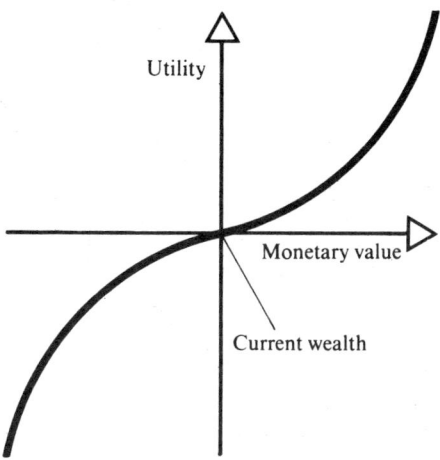

Figure 4. Utility function for money consistent with insurance purchase and gambling behaviour

Why is it necessary to go through the lottery ticket procedure to determine an individual's utility for money? Why isn't utility for money assessed directly in an analogous way to probability? Look back at the monetary values you attached to 50 and 100 utiles. £10,000 should be exactly twice as desirable as the amount of money you equated with 50 utiles. You have probably equated less monetary value to 50 utiles than now seems reasonable. As Edwards has noted,

> . . . it would require a lot of evidence to convince many researchers that subjects, asked how much money is half as desirable as $10, would systematically answer something different from $5. The numerical properties of money may be far more important in deter-

mining responses than their utility properties, no matter what instructions are given.'[7]

Of course, a monetary outcome isn't the only possible consequence of a decision; indeed, monetary values are often not involved in decision-making. Such choices may involve the assessment of *multi-attributed utility*. Consider my decision to purchase a car. Suppose I have limited my choice to three cars: a Volkswagen Polo, a Ford Escort and a Rover 3500. Table 2 sets out the attributes, or part-worths, of the total utility, or total worth, *I* attach to each alternative car. Several methods are currently used to elicit the attributes for evaluation. One method developed by Humphreys and Humphreys[8] makes triad comparisons of the form: how are alternative B *and* alternative C similar and yet different from alternative A? The dimensions of difference are then used as the attributes for evaluation of the alternatives. Statistical tests are used to test the independence of the attributes so that redundant attributes, e.g. acceleration and performance, which would bias choice by over-representation of a psychologically similar attribute, are selectively eliminated.

Once the attributes for evaluation have been identified it is now

Table 2. Multi-attributed utility decomposition for my choice of car

Decomposition		Car Alternatives		
		Volkswagen Polo	Ford Escort	Rover 3500
Attribute weights	Attributes	Attribute scores	Attribute scores	Attribute scores
10	Speed	50	70	100
5	Comfort	40	60	100
45	Price	100	90	10
20	Depreciation	100	80	10
20	Miles per Gallon	100	80	10

necessary to weight their relative importance. For instance, in choice of cars, price may be a very important attribute whereas comfort is of much less importance. Again, several methods exist for the elicitation of the attribute weights. Edwards[9] recommends first a rank ordering of the attributes in terms of their importance and then a translation of the rankings into relative weightings, such that if an attribute is given a weighting of 20 it should be considered four times as important as an attribute with a weighting of 5. Once weightings are elicited they can be 'normalized' to sum to 100.

Once the attribute weightings are assessed, each alternative must now be measured or scored on the attribute dimensions. As with the measurement of utility for money, the zero point and unit of measurement are arbitrary, but it is conventional to use a scale which extends from 0 to 100. As with the weighting of the attributes, the scores on the attributes should be relative scores. In my choice problem I have given the Volkswagen Polo a score of 100 on depreciation and a Rover 3500 only 10; I consider the depreciation of the Polo to be 10 times better than that of the Rover.

Once the attributes of the alternative choices have been elicited, their importance weighted and the alternatives scored on the attributes, we are in a position to evaluate the alternatives. Multi-attributed utility theory (MAUT) specifies that the total utility or worth of an alternative is the sum of scores on the weighted attribute dimensions. Let's calculate my assessed worth for each of the three alternative cars.

Volkswagen Polo $U = (50 \times 10) + (40 \times 5) + (100 \times 45) + (100 \times 20) + (100 \times 20) = \mathbf{9{,}200}$ utiles

Ford Escort $U = (70 \times 10) + (60 \times 5) + (90 \times 45) + (80 \times 20) + (80 \times 20) = \mathbf{8{,}250}$ utiles

Rover 3500 $U = (100 \times 10) + (100 \times 5) + (10 \times 45) + (10 \times 20) + (10 \times 20) = \mathbf{2{,}350}$ utiles.

I'll buy the Polo!

In this example my intuitive or holistic utilities for the alternative cars don't conflict with the MAUT specified preferences. What if there was a conflict? In an analogous way to SEU theory and Bayes' theorem (to be described later) MAUT is a normative theory of choice based on certain axioms or principles. If you, as the decision-maker, accept the axioms of MAUT then you should follow the preferences specified by MAUT, even if they conflict with your intuitive preference orderings.

Another source of validation for the MAUT approach is the finding

Behavioral Decision Theory

that when there are only a few attributes involved in a choice between alternatives, the within-person correlations between MAUT specified and intuitive preference orderings are high and positive. However, as the number of attributes increases, the strength of the correlations between the two preference orderings decreases.[10] A related topic, multi-attributed inference, which also has bearing on the acceptance of MAUT as a normative theory of choice, is discussed in Chapter 6.

Why don't MAUT prescribed preference orderings and intuitive preference orderings always agree? Explanations of the cause of this conflict generally invoke the notion of the 'limited information processing capacity' of the human decision-maker who is unable to perform all the multiplications and additions required by a MAUT analysis, although the decision-maker is able to provide the necessary inputs to a MAUT analysis. A similar argument was used by Howard Raiffa in his defence of decision analysis: 'Decision analysis improves decision-making by dividing and conquering.'

The notion that 'limited information processing capacity' causes suboptimal decision-making has also been used to explain the limits and biases to which human judgement has been shown to be subject. This research will now be described in detail.

Limitations and Biases in Human Judgement

How do people assess probabilities? Tversky and Kahneman, in a series of papers,[11] have outlined some of the heuristics, or rules of thumb, that people tend to use in the assessment of the likelihood of events. To illustrate their findings I will present two questions which I would like you to answer.

1. Suppose I sample a word of three letters or more at random from an English text. Is it more likely that the word starts with an 'r' or that 'r' is its third letter?
2. Which cause of death is more likely out of each pair:
    i) Lung cancer *or* stomach cancer
    ii) Murder *or* suicide
    iii) Diabetes *or* a motor vehicle accident?

Now for the answers! If you are like most of Tversky and Kahneman's subjects you may have said that 'r' is more likely to start a word. However, in reality, 'r' is more frequent as the third letter. Tversky and

Estimation of Probability and Utility

Kahneman argue that people approach the problem by recalling words that begin with an 'r', e.g. road, railway, and words that have 'r' as the third letter, e.g. care. Because it is much easier to search for words by their first letter than by their third letter most people, Tversky and Kahneman argue, judge that words beginning with 'r' are more likely.

Tversky and Kahneman have also demonstrated that we often judge the probability of an event by the ease with which relevant information of that event is imagined. Instances of frequent events are typically easier to recall than instances of less frequent events, thus *availability* is often a valid cue for the assessment of frequency and probability. However, since availability is also influenced by factors unrelated to likelihood, such as familiarity, recency and emotional saliency, reliance on it may result in systematic biases. In a convincing study, Lichtenstein *et al.*[12] found that people overestimated the relative frequency of diseases or causes of death which are much publicized, such as murder or lung cancer, whereas the relative frequency of less publicized causes of death, such as stomach cancer and diabetes, were underestimated. In all parts of question 2 above, the second alternative is about one and a half times more likely than the first alternative. Most people think that death by lung cancer is much more likely than death by stomach cancer and death by murder is much more likely than suicide. Conversely, most people think that death by motor vehicle accident is many more times likely than death caused by diabetes.

Another heuristic that tends to bias probabilistic judgement is *representativeness*. Consider the following problem adapted from Tversky and Kahneman.

> This is a brief personality description of Tom W. written by a psychologist when Tom was in his senior year at high school:
> Tom W. is of high intelligence, although lacking in true creativity. He has a need for order and clarity and for neat and tidy systems in which every detail finds its appropriate place. His writing is rather dull and mechanical, occasionally enlivened by somewhat corny puns and by flashes of imagination of the sci-fi type. He has a strong drive for competence. He seems to have little feel and little sympathy for other people and does not enjoy interacting with others. Self-centred, he nonetheless has a deep moral sense. This personality description has been chosen, at random, from those of 30 engineers and 70 social scientists. What is your probability that Tom W. is an engineer? __ __ __ __

Behavioral Decision Theory

You have probably answered that Tom W. is more likely to be an engineer than a social scientist. However, Tversky and Kahneman argue that the base rate should have predominance over the low-reliability personality sketch, such that your probability response should be little different, if at all, from the base-rate probability of a 0·7 chance that Tom W. is a social scientist. Using similar problems Tversky and Kahneman found that when no individuating evidence is given, base rates are properly utilized, but when worthless information is given, as in the above example, base rates are ignored. Tversky and Kahneman coined the term *representativeness* to refer to the dominance of individuating information in intuitive prediction. A normative method for the combination of base-rate information with additional information is presented in Chapter 5, where we will discuss the issue of sub-optimality in opinion revision in more detail.

Tversky and Kahneman have also identified a heuristic called *anchoring and adjustment*. To demonstrate this effect, subjects were asked to estimate various quantities, stated in percentages (e.g. the percentage of African countries in the United Nations). Before they made their estimates, the subjects were shown an arbitrary starting value between 0 and 100 given by the result of a spin of a wheel of fortune. Subjects were required to indicate whether they considered this value too high or too low and then to give their own estimate. Different groups of people were given different starting values. Surprisingly, the arbitrary starting values had a considerable influence on estimation. For example, median estimates for the question posed above were 25 per cent and 45 per cent, for groups which received 10 per cent and 65 per cent as starting points, respectively. Reward for accuracy did not reduce the anchoring and adjustment effect.

Slovic[13] gave another example of anchoring in the subjective valuation of gambles. He found that in making these judgements people who find a gamble basically attractive use the amount to win as a natural starting point. They then adjust the amount to win downward to take into account the less-than-perfect chance of winning and the possibility of losing a small amount. Typically, this adjustment is insufficient and Slovic argued that this is why people *price* gambles inconsistently with straight choices between pairs of gambles where a monetary response is not required.

Another bias in probability estimation that has been known to exist for a long time is the 'gamblers' fallacy'. Dostoevsky[14] observed that in roulette '... after the red has come up ten times in a row, hardly

Estimation of Probability and Utility

anyone will persist in betting on it'. This belief that the black is more likely to come up after a long run of red is fallacious: the roulette ball has no memory! Consider the results of two sequences of tossing a coin.

Sequence 1   T T T T T H H H H
Sequence 2   H T T H T H H T T

Which sequence is more likely to be the result of the throwing of a 'fair' coin? Most people would, I think, consider sequence 2 to be the result of throwing a fair coin. However, one law of probability to be discussed in chapter 5 states that 'the probability of both event A and event B occurring is equal to the probability of A multiplied by the probability of B, *given* that event A has occurred'. In this problem the throws of the coin are independent events and so any occurrence of a head has no effect on the probability of a tail. Therefore it follows that the probability that sequence 1 is the result of a sequence of nine throws is identical to the probability that sequence 2 is the result of a sequence of nine throws. This is because both sequences contain four heads and five tails. In other words both sequences are equally likely to have been the result of throwing the *same* coin.

Yet another bias in judgement has been identified as *misperception of regression towards the mean*. Suppose a large number of children have been given an intelligence test. Some children scored above the mean, some below. If an equivalent test was then administered to the children, those children who scored above the mean on the first test would obtain a lower average score on the second test, whereas those children who scored below the mean on the first test would obtain a higher average score on the second test. Random fluctuations around the mean will produce sub-standard and above-standard performance which is highly likely to be followed by an improvement and a worsening respectively. This phenomenon, known as *regression towards the mean*, was first documented by Galton a century ago. Failure to understand the importance of regression can have important consequences, as Tversky and Kahneman have documented. They found that flight instructors typically praised the trainee pilot after the successful execution of a flight manoeuvre and admonished him after a poor performance. Lack of understanding of regression towards the mean led the flight instructors to the erroneous conclusion that praise is detrimental to learning whereas punishment is beneficial. Tversky and Kahneman argue that people tend to use causal explanations to explain random variation.

Tversky and Kahneman have devised many simple paper and pencil tests that have revealed heuristics people commonly use when making judgements about uncertain events. According to Tversky and Kahneman these heuristic principles may be quite useful in that they reduce the complexity of probability estimation, but they can lead to severe and systematic errors, analogous to the effects of the perceptual illusions. For example, perceptual psychology has documented that one cue to distance evaluation is the clarity of an object's image on the retina. The sharper the image of an object, the closer it appears to be. Clarity as a cue to distance has obvious general validity. However, when visibility is poor, distances are overestimated because the contours of an object are indistinct. Similarly, when visibility is good, distance is underestimated.

How can the biases of the heuristic principles be reduced so that the process of probability estimation is improved? In a paper entitled 'Intuitive prediction: Biases and corrective procedures'[15] Kahneman and Tversky have attempted to answer this question. Their 'strategy of debiasing' essentially concentrates on the elicitation and recognition of the importance of the usually neglected, but otherwise available, base-rate information for use in prediction. However, I think it is fair to say that, although the heuristics and biases which influence probability assessment have become documented increasingly over the last decade, methods for the elicitation of unbiased assessment have only recently become the subject of research. If the heuristics and biases are similar to perceptual illusions, as Tversky and Kahneman suggest, awareness of the causes of a judgemental illusion is, by itself, not likely to reduce the illusory effect.

Realism of Assessed Probabilities

The previous sections have shown that subjective probability assessments, although generally reliable, can be subject to possible biases such as availability, representativeness, anchoring and adjustment, misconceptions of chance, and misconceptions of regression. Another approach to the question of the validity of probability assessments has been an interest in realism or 'calibration'. A person is said to be perfectly calibrated if, for all events or propositions to which he or she assigns a given subjective probability (P), the proportion that occurs,

Estimation of Probability and Utility

or is correct, is P. For example, if you assign a probability of 0·7 to each of ten questions concerning the possible occurrence of future events, you should get seven of those questions correct. Similarly, all events that you assess as being certain to occur (1·0 probability assessments) should, in fact, occur.

The relation between assessed probability and hit rate that would be obtained by a perfectly calibrated person is represented by the diagonal line in Figure 5.

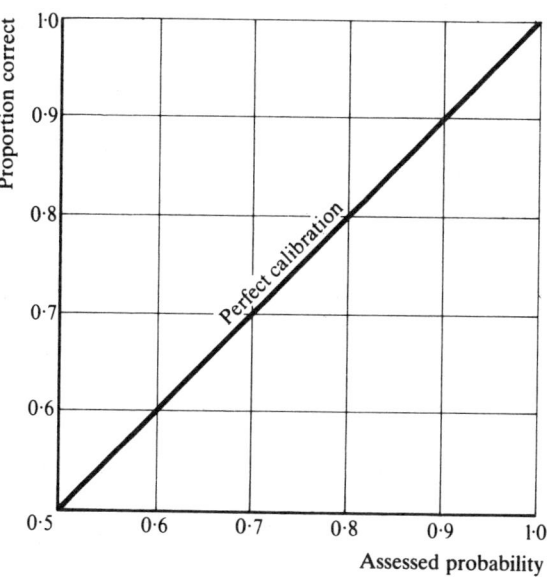

Figure 5. A perfectly calibrated person

Most studies of calibration have used general knowledge questions instead of future event questions because the answers can be immediately evaluated by the experimenter.

Let's see how calibrated your probabilities are. Below are thirty questions with two possible answers, one of which is correct, for example:

Where does the sun rise?

(a) West
(b) East

Behavioral Decision Theory

Indicate your answer by circling the appropriate letter, for example:

(a) West
((b)) East

On the line to the right of the answers, indicate how sure you are in probability terms.

(a) West
(b) East _____ probability

The scale for probability extends from 0·5 to 1·0, with 1·0 meaning absolutely sure and 0·5 meaning completely unsure. Note that even if you had absolutely no idea what the correct answer was, you would still have a 0·5 chance of being correct as there are only two alternatives. For most of the questions your probability will probably lie between the extremes, that is, you won't be absolutely sure, nor will you be completely unsure. You would therefore select some point between 0·5 and 1·0 to indicate how sure you were. For ease of scoring please use only assessments of 0·5, 0·6, 0·7, 0·8, 0·9 and 1·0.

QUESTIONS

1. Which is nearer London? (a) New York
   (b) Moscow _____

2. Who 'discovered' New Zealand? (a) Abel Tasman
   (b) Captain Cook _____

3. When did the Peoples' Republic of China join the UN? (a) 1972
   (b) 1971 _____

4. Which legs do cows use first when getting up from the ground? (a) Hind legs
   (b) Front legs _____

5. Which is the smallest country in South America? (a) Ecuador
   (b) Uruguay _____

6. Where was Frank Sinatra born? (a) Sicily
   (b) USA _____

7. Which is longer? (a) Panama Canal
   (b) Suez Canal _____

Estimation of Probability and Utility

8. Which was 'discovered' first?
   - (a) Einstein's Theory of Relativity
   - (b) Aspirin _____

9. Which tropic is north of the Equator?
   - (a) Capricorn
   - (b) Cancer _____

10. When were the modern Olympic Games started?
    - (a) Nineteenth century
    - (b) Twentieth century _____

11. Which is heavier?
    - (a) Carbon Dioxide
    - (b) Air _____

12. Which camel has two humps?
    - (a) Bactrian
    - (b) Arabian _____

13. What is the capital of New Zealand?
    - (a) Auckland
    - (b) Wellington _____

14. Who launched the first satellite?
    - (a) United States
    - (b) USSR _____

15. Which country produces more natural rubber?
    - (a) Brazil
    - (b) Malaya _____

16. Which does Japan produce more of (by weight)?
    - (a) Wheat
    - (b) Rice _____

17. Which was formed first?
    - (a) South-East Asia Treaty Organization
    - (b) North Atlantic Treaty Organization _____

18. Biennial means
    - (a) Twice a year
    - (b) Once every two years _____

19. The average gestation period for elephants is
    - (a) Over one year
    - (b) Under one year _____

20. Aladdin's nationality was
    - (a) Chinese
    - (b) Japanese _____

21. Where are the Atlas Mountains?
    - (a) Europe
    - (b) Africa _____

22. Which country has the larger land area?
    - (a) USSR
    - (b) China _____

23. Which is larger in terms of surface area?
    - (a) Atlantic Ocean
    - (b) Pacific Ocean _____

Behavioral Decision Theory

24. Which type of vessels carry blood from the heart?
    (a) Artery
    (b) Vein
    _____

25. Which civilization came first?
    (a) Greek
    (b) Roman
    _____

26. Which metal is denser?
    (a) Iron
    (b) Copper
    _____

27. Which contains more proteins per unit weight?
    (a) Eggs
    (b) Steak (beef)
    _____

28. Did the USSR and Denmark or did
    (a) Join the UN at the same time
    (b) the USSR join first?
    _____

29. Which has the greater average life expectancy?
    (a) Elephant
    (b) Man
    _____

30. Which is larger?
    (a) Black Sea
    (b) Caspian Sea
    _____

The correct answers are printed in Appendix 1 (p. 117). Now, for all similar assessments, work out your proportion correct.

$$\text{Proportion correct for 0·5 responses} = \frac{\text{how many 0·5 responses were correct}}{\text{how many 0·5 responses you gave}}$$

Repeat the calculation for any 0·6, 0·7, 0·8, 0·9 and 1·0 assessments that you gave and then plot proportion correct for each group of similar assessments on the grid in Figure 5. Draw a line to connect sequential points to form a graph. You'll probably find that you aren't perfectly calibrated. Most likely the majority of points on your 'calibration curve' will lie below the diagonal indicating that you are *overconfident*. In other words your proportion correct for each group of assessed probabilities may be *less* than your assessed probability.

Figure 6 gives examples of overconfident and underconfident calibration curves based on grouped data. Your calibration curve may not look exactly like either of these typical curves because your curve is based on only 30 probability assessments and you may have made only a few assessments at some probability levels. Lichtenstein and Fischhoff have conducted an extensive programme of studies on the calibration of subjective probabilities. Their general finding is that most of the time most people are overconfident in probability assessment,

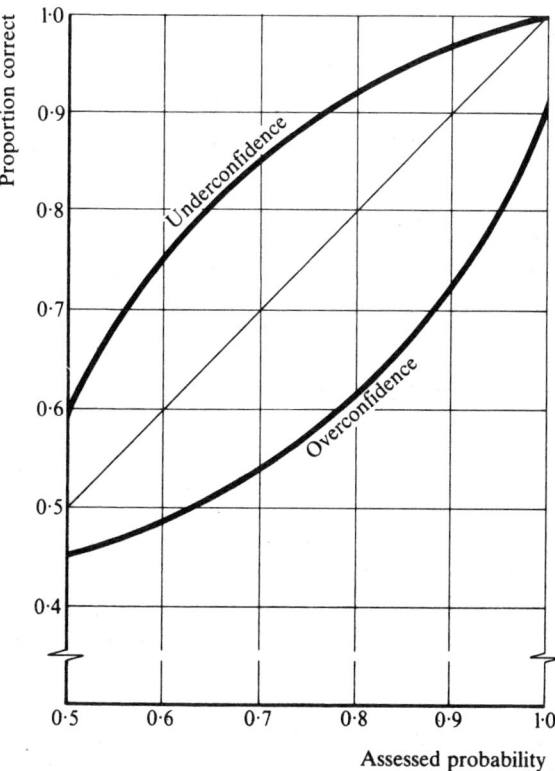

Figure 6. Overconfidence and underconfidence

especially with difficult questions.[16] Their measure of difficulty is simply the overall proportion correct. To calculate this simply divide the number of questions you answered correctly by the total number of questions, i.e. 30. Lichtenstein and Fischhoff found that as the difficulty measure drops below 0·8 people become more overconfident, whereas when the questions are found to become increasingly easy, i.e. a difficulty measure of above 0·8, people become more underconfident. This empirical finding has been duplicated many times with different questions and using a wide variety of subjects. Intelligence does not appear to affect calibration scores, nor does an odds or probability response mode.

Several studies have investigated the effect of training to improve calibration. Training has involved feedback of calibration curves and discussion of the concept of calibration. However, only modest transfer of training to new sets of items has been achieved, possibly because of changes in difficulty of item sets. Recently, Koriat et al.[17] have demonstrated that calibration improved when subjects were required to list reasons for and against their answers. Listing of negative reasons produced a decrease in overconfidence and thus an improvement in calibration. This line of research is still continuing, but it does appear that one reason for overconfidence is the failure to generate negative evidence.

Why aren't we better calibrated? Why don't we learn from experience? Fischhoff and Beyeth[18] have found that when decision-makers are told which event actually occurred and are then asked to recall their original subjective probabilities, most decision-makers exhibit the 'I knew it all along effect'. Recalled probability is nearer 1·0 (or certainty) than the *original* probability estimate.

Given the validity of SEU theory as a normative method for decision-making, an improvement in ability to assess well-calibrated probabilities will logically improve the overall quality of a person's decision-making. Chapter 4 extends the discussion of calibration and, more generally, probabilistic thinking, and offers evidence that an ability to express and utilize probabilistic information is highly situation specific. It may well be impossible to select good general decision-makers.

Summary

This chapter has reviewed some of the methods that can be used to elicit the subjective probabilities and utilities required for an SEU analysis. Inconsistency between methods and the reliability of single methods were discussed but no firm conclusions about best methods for probability or utility measurement can, at present, be drawn. Individual differences in the utility attached to money were demonstrated and multi-attributed utility theory was introduced as a normative choice principle.

Subjective probability assessments were shown to be subject to such heuristics and biases as availability, representativeness, anchoring and adjustment, misconceptions of chance, and misconceptions of regression. Although a large number of heuristics and biases have now been documented, methods for debiasing assessments are still under development. Finally, calibration was introduced as one method for measuring the validity of probability assessments.

3 Does Subjective Expected Utility Theory Describe Decision-making?

This chapter presents an overview of research that has investigated whether SEU describes choice decisions between simple gambles and between more complex 'duplex' gambles. Finally, research that has questioned the normative status of SEU, by testing the acceptability of the sure-thing principle, is evaluated.

Choice between Simple Gambles

Consider the pair of gambles presented in Figure 1. Which gamble do

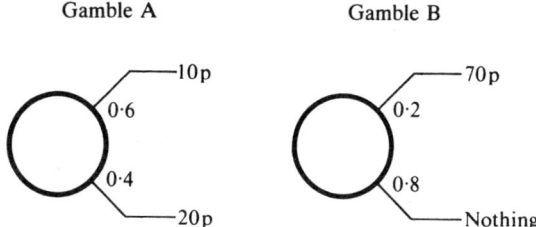

Figure 1. Two simple gambles

you prefer, gamble A or gamble B? If you are similar to one of Ward Edwards's subjects you will have chosen gamble B over gamble A, reasoning that if you do not stand much chance of losing anything you prefer a long shot to win a reasonable amount rather than the certainty of winning only a small amount. However, if we work out the *expected value* (EV) of each of the two gambles, they are equivalent:

For gamble A: $(0\cdot6 \times 10p) + (0\cdot4 \times 20p) = $ **14**
For gamble B: $(0\cdot2 \times 70p) + (0\cdot8 \times 0p) = $ **14**

If we assume that the stated probabilities given in the problem are equivalent to your *subjective* probabilities, and your utilities for the payoffs in the gambles are equivalent to the stated monetary values, then it follows from SEU theory that you should be *indifferent* – in other words, you should have no preference for one gamble over the other. Are these two assumptions reasonable? Well, you have no reason to suppose I am lying when I gave you the probabilities, and for such small amounts of money it may be reasonable to assume that utility and value are equivalent, i.e., 70p is worth seven times as much to you as 10p.

In a series of experiments Edwards[1] demonstrated that two thirds of his sample of people had definite preferences between pairs of gambles that had equivalent expected values.[2] Specifically, he argued that most people had *probability preferences* in that they preferred gambles containing long shots of winning large amounts provided that there was little or no chance of losing very much. However, most of his sample of people also avoided gambles that involved even a low probability of losing a lot. Edwards concluded that for most people expected value was not a guide to choosing between gambles. In a later study, Lichtenstein, Slovic and Zinc[3] found that expected value was irrelevant as a guide to choice *even when the concept was carefully explained*.

The results of these two studies were initial evidence that SEU may not be *descriptive* of human decision-making in choices between simple gambles. However, this research, and the research to be described below, makes no statement about the *normative* status of SEU as the optimal decision principle.

Lichtenstein and Slovic[4] had subjects evaluate gambles, similar in nature to those shown in Figure 1, by a choice procedure and also by a bidding procedure. The choice procedure required subjects to indicate which of a pair of gambles they preferred whilst the bidding procedure asked subjects to name an amount of money at which they would be indifferent between playing a specified single gamble or having that amount of money. When they compared the results of the choice and bidding procedures they found, surprisingly, that for the same subject the results of the two procedures were not correlated. Specifically, they often found that subjects would indicate a greater preference for one gamble when a choice procedure was used, and bid more for another gamble when a bidding procedure was used. When asked to choose between gambles, people tended to prefer those containing a higher probability of winning, whereas higher bids were made

Does Subjective Expected Utility Theory Describe Decision-making?

for gambles containing the larger amounts to win. These results are clearly inconsistent with the SEU theory of decision-making, used descriptively, which would specify that all choices should be made by maximizing SEU.

This response-mode effect was confirmed on the floor of the Four Queens Casino in Las Vegas, suggesting that the effect will generalize to people other than the average university undergraduate, the usual participant in most psychology experiments! For the two bets shown in Figure 2, A and B were preferred about equally often by Lichten-

GAMBLE A | GAMBLE B
$\frac{11}{12}$ chance to win 12 chips | $\frac{2}{12}$ chance to win 79 chips
$\frac{1}{12}$ chance to win 24 chips | $\frac{10}{12}$ chance to lose 5 chips

where each chip could represent either $0.1, $1 or $5.

Figure 2. Two simple gambles used by Lichtenstein and Slovic

stein and Slovic's sample of casino subjects. However, gamble B was given a higher monetary value about 88 per cent of the time. Of the subjects who preferred gamble A, 87 per cent gave a higher monetary value to gamble B, thus showing an inconsistent preference pattern.

What could account for this inconsistency? Subjects seemed to prefer gamble A because of its good odds but set a higher monetary value on gamble B because of its large winning payoff. Slovic[5] has argued that a 'compatibility' effect is operating. Since a monetary valuation is expressed in terms of money, subjects found it easier to use the monetary aspect of the gamble to set the value of the gamble. When subjects are simply asked which of two gambles they prefer they have no reason to use potential payoffs as a starting point or 'anchor'. When the inconsistency of their decisions was pointed out to the subjects of the experiment, they put up considerable resistance to changing their inconsistent responses. However, as Slovic pointed out, 'strict adherence to an inconsistent pattern of prices and choices can be termed "irrational", since the inconsistent subject can be made to become a "money-pump", easily led into purchasing and trading gambles in such a way that he continually loses money'.

In another study using simple two-outcome gambles Tversky[6] varied the probabilities of winning from $\frac{7}{24}$ to $\frac{11}{24}$ in increments of $\frac{1}{24}$, while the associated payoffs ranged from $4 to $5 in increments of $0.25. He

Behavioral Decision Theory

found that when the probability differences between gambles were small, subjects tended to choose on the basis of amount to win, while when the probability differences were increased people tended to choose on the basis of the probabilities. By a careful manipulation of the gambles Tversky showed intransitivity of preferences which were clearly inconsistent with the descriptive adequacy of the transitivity axiom of SEU.

Well, if SEU does not describe choices between simple gambles, what factors influence choice? Clearly, as we have seen, some psychological translation of the probabilities and payoffs involved in a gamble has an influence on choice. However, other investigators have argued that the *variance*, or dispersion, of the probabilities and payoffs has a stronger influence on choice than the probabilities and payoffs *per se*. Consider the pair of two-outcome gambles presented in Figure 3.

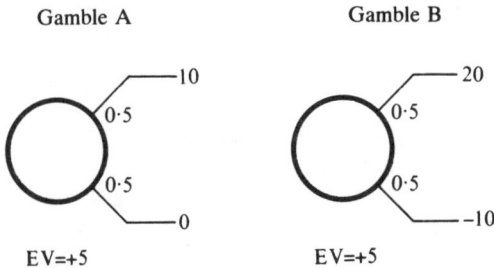

Figure 3. Two simple gambles with similar expected values and stated probabilities

Both have the same expected value and stated probabilities. However, as you will see from Figure 4, the dispersion of the payoffs is much greater in gamble B than in gamble A. More formally, the variance of a two-outcome gamble is calculated as $PQ(X-Y)^2$ where P is the probability associated with outcome X and Q is the probability associated with outcome Y.

In our case, the variance of gamble A is $0.25 (10)^2 = 25$, while the variance of gamble B is $0.25 (30)^2 = 225$. In other words the variance of gamble B is nine times as much as that of gamble A.

Another way to describe differences between two-outcome gambles is in terms of their skewness, or lopsidedness, around the zero payoff.

Does Subjective Expected Utility Theory Describe Decision-making?

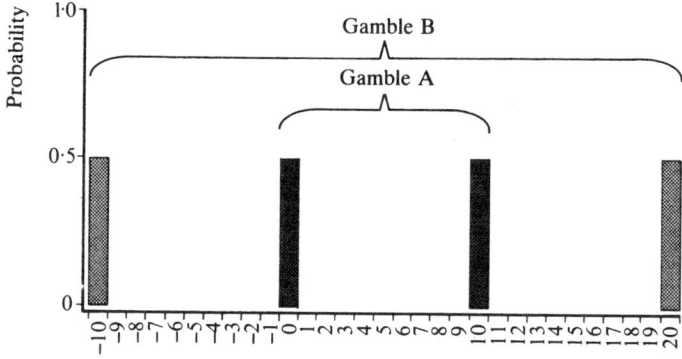

Figure 4. The dispersion of payoffs for the two gambles shown in Figure 3

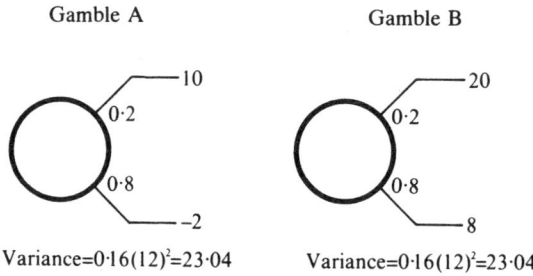

Figure 5. A pair of two-outcome gambles with similar variances and stated probabilities

Consider the pair of two-outcome gambles presented in Figure 5. They both have the same stated probabilities and the same variances but gamble B is skewed much more to the right of a zero payoff than gamble A. The dispersion of the payoffs for the two gambles is given in Figure 6.

Coombs and Pruitt[7] have argued that the variance and skewness of a gamble contribute to its perceived 'riskiness'. In their experiment they systematically varied EV, variance and skewness and found that subjects had both variance and skewness preferences. About one third

55

Behavioral Decision Theory

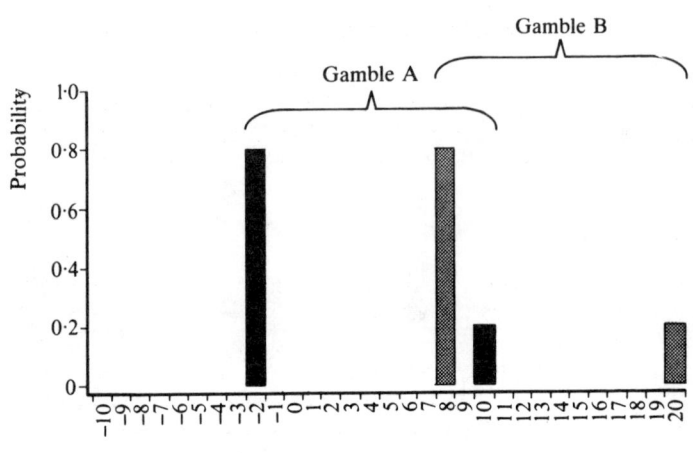

Figure 6. The dispersion of the payoffs for the two gambles shown in Figure 5

of their subjects had a preference for high variance gambles, one third preferred intermediate variance gambles, while the remaining third preferred low variance gambles. Similarly, there were individual differences in preferred level of skewness.

Their results led Coombs and Pruitt to suggest an alternative *description* of choice behaviour to contrast with SEU theory. They argued that, while people will always be guided by SEU, individuals also have a utility for risk, which will show itself as a preference for certain amounts of variance or skewness. Coombs has extended this early research result into his portfolio theory of choice, which will be described in detail in Chapter 6. For now we note that his findings are inconsistent with SEU as a descriptive theory of choice behaviour.

However, one study by Sarah Lichtenstein[8] contradicted Coombs and Pruitt's results. Using real monetary payoffs, instead of the imaginary ones used by Coombs and Pruitt, she found that most of her subjects preferred low variance bets and that the skewness of a gamble had no effect on choice. She reconciled the inconsistency between her study and that of Coombs and Pruitt by arguing that her subject may have had a real fear of losing money and so avoided her riskier, high variance bets.

Does Subjective Expected Utility Theory Describe Decision-making?

One recent review of the literature sums up the research very succinctly:

'Expected value, variance, probabilities of winning and losing, and other transformations of two-outcome gambles all affect the perceived riskiness of gambles in one way or another . . .'[9]

Choice between Complex Gambles

The above approaches to developing a descriptive theory of choice between simple gambles have tested the descriptive relevance of various mathematical manipulations of the probabilities and payoffs inherent in the gambles. By contrast, other studies by Slovic and Lichtenstein have taken a more psychological information processing approach, in which a descriptive decision theory is developed *subsequent* to subjects' choices between the gambles.

Much of Slovic and Lichtenstein's research has used 'duplex gambles' instead of the simplest two-outcome gambles we described earlier. This was because it is extremely difficult to manipulate experimentally a single attribute of a two-outcome gamble independently of its other attributes. Consider the two gambles shown in Figure 5; their variances and stated probabilities are equivalent but four attributes differ – skewness, EV, amount to win and amount to lose. Duplex gambles, on the other hand, are much easier to manipulate, *but* they are, at least initially, much more difficult to comprehend. Consider the duplex gamble shown in Figure 7. Imagine that the circular discs each have a spinnable pointer attached, which I, as the

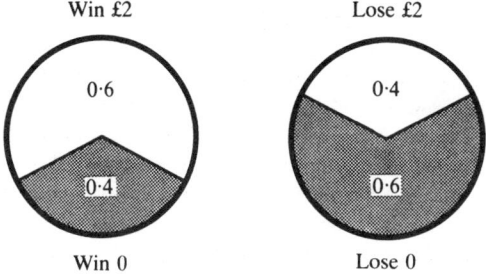

Figure 7. A duplex gamble

Behavioral Decision Theory

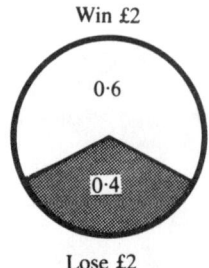

Figure 8. The parallel standard gamble to the duplex gamble shown in Figure 7

experimenter, am about to flick and set in motion. Whichever portion of the disc the pointer comes to rest in, you win or lose the amount shown. To play the duplex bet I will spin the pointer on both discs. Thus, you can win and not lose, lose and not win, both win and lose or neither win or lose. Next, consider what Slovic and Lichtenstein call the 'parallel standard gamble', presented in Figure 8.

To play the standard gamble I will spin the pointer and you either win or lose.

Now, which do you prefer? The duplex gamble in Figure 7 or the parallel standard gamble in Figure 8? If you are similar to Slovic and Lichtenstein's subjects you will have rated the two sets of gamble as equally attractive. However, consider the distribution of payoffs attached to the two types of gambles, shown in Figure 9.

The variance of a duplex gamble is calculated as $PQ(X^2 + Y^2)$, which in our case is $0.24 (2^2 + 2^2) = 1.92$; while the variance of the parallel standard gamble is calculated as $PQ(X - Y)^2$, which is $0.24 (2 + 2)^2 = 3.84$. So, the variance of the standard gamble is twice that of the duplex gamble. Using a wide variety of duplex gambles and equivalent standard gambles Slovic and Lichtenstein[10] found that most people were indifferent between the sets of two gambles. These results led them to argue that judgements about gambles are based only on the *explicitly* displayed probabilities and payoffs. The underlying variance and skewness of gambles has no influence on judgement, at least with these complex gambles.

In a complementary study conducted by Payne and Braunstein,[11] pairs of duplex gambles were designed to have equal variance and

Does Subjective Expected Utility Theory Describe Decision-making?

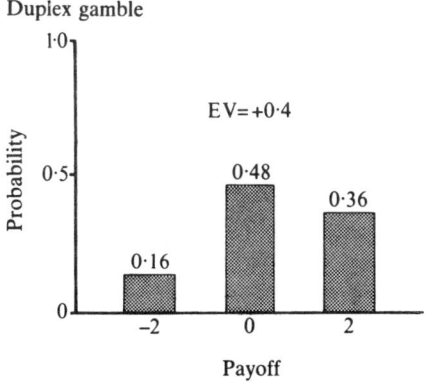

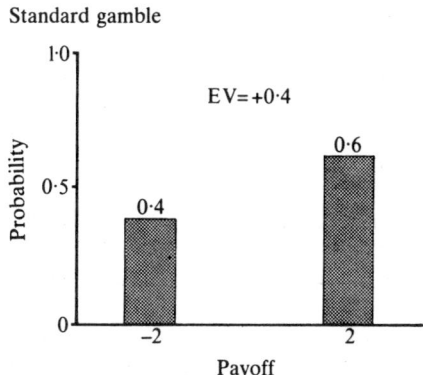

Figure 9. Distribution of payoffs attached to the duplex gamble and its parallel standard gamble

skewness *but* different explicitly displayed probabilities. An example is given in Figure 10.

Payne and Braunstein found that most of the subjects of their experiment had definite preferences for one duplex gamble over the other. The results from the duplex gamble research, *taken together*, support the notion that when people make judgements about fairly complex gambles they make them only in terms of the *explicit* probabilities of winning or losing, and the explicit amounts to win and to lose, rather than on the *implicit* variance and skewness *or* SEU.

Behavioral Decision Theory

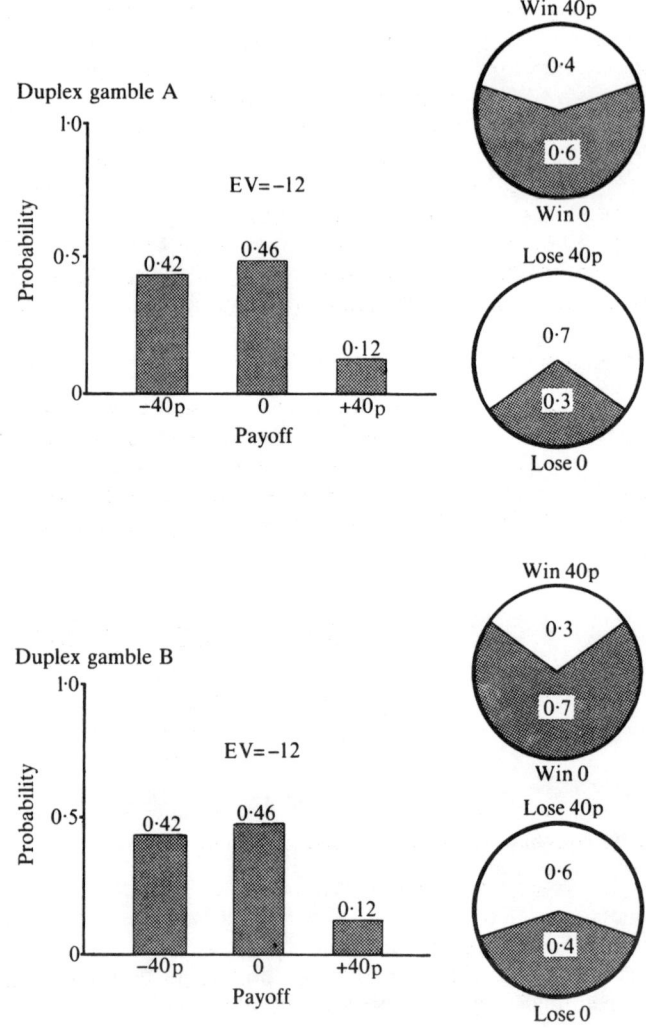

Figure 10. Pairs of duplex gambles with equal variance but different explicitly displayed probabilities

From P. Slovic, 'From Shakespeare to Simon: Speculations – and some evidence – about man's ability to process information' (see note 5). Adapted by permission of the author.

Does Subjective Expected Utility Theory Describe Decision-making?

From their findings Slovic and Lichtenstein derived an alternative descriptive model of risky decision-making. This will be described in detail in Chapter 6. For the moment we conclude that the findings of the duplex bet research are inconsistent with SEU as a *description* of human choice behaviour in uncertain situations. This research says nothing about the normative status of SEU and perhaps could be taken by itself as evidence for the need to develop decision analysis in order to help people make better decisions.

Next we will review studies that have investigated the *acceptability* of the sure-thing axiom I outlined earlier. In the decision theory literature the results of these studies have been termed 'paradoxical'.

Tests of the Acceptability of an Axiom of SEU

Ellsberg's[12] test of the acceptability of the sure-thing principle is shown in Figure 11. Imagine an opaque bag known to contain ninety balls. Thirty of the balls are red, the remaining sixty are black or yellow in unknown proportions. One ball is to be drawn at random from the bag. Look at Figure 11 and consider the following actions and outcomes.

	30	60	
	Red	*Black*	*Yellow*
Situation A			
Act 1: Bet on red	£10	Nothing	Nothing
Act 2: Bet on black	Nothing	£10	Nothing
Situation B			
Act 3: Bet on red or yellow	£10	Nothing	£10
Act 4: Bet on black or yellow	Nothing	£10	£10

Figure 11. Ellsberg's test of the sure-thing principle

In situation A, if you bet on red, act 1, you will win £10 if a red ball is drawn. If you bet on black, act 2, you will win £10 if a black ball is drawn and nothing if a red or yellow ball is drawn.

Next, consider the two possible actions in situation B. Here, if you bet on red or yellow, act 3, you will win £10 if either a red or yellow ball is drawn and win nothing if black is drawn. If you choose act 4, you win £10 if either a black or yellow ball is drawn and win nothing if red is drawn.

Behavioral Decision Theory

Now re-read Figure 11 and choose between act 1 and act 2 *and* between act 3 and act 4 by marking with a pencil the act you most prefer in each situation.

If you have chosen in a similar way to the subjects of Ellsberg's experiments you will have chosen act 1 in situation A, by reasoning that at least you know that there are thirty reds, whereas in act 2 there could be less than thirty blacks. In situation B you will have chosen act 4, reasoning that at least sixty of the balls are either black or yellow, whereas in act 3 there may be less than sixty red and yellow balls.

But consider the event of a yellow ball being picked at random from the opaque bag. In situation A both available acts have a common outcome: you win nothing. Similarly, in situation B, the common outcome for yellow is a £10 win. Now recall the sure-thing principle: 'when you are in the process of making a choice between possible acts, the outcomes that are not related to your choice should not influence your choice'. Surely it follows that situation A and situation B are identical in terms of the information to be utilized in a decision between the pairs of acts? In other words if you choose act 1 in situation A you should choose act 3 in situation B. Alternatively, a choice of act 2 should be followed by a choice of act 4.

Perhaps you do not agree; you may have noticed that some of the probabilities involved in Ellsberg's paradox are *ambiguous*. For instance, you are told only that sixty of the balls are either black *or* yellow but not the proportion of black to yellow. This is true *but*, by what is called a *symmetry argument*, it can be inferred that the proportion of black and yellow balls are equal because there is no evidence to the contrary.

You may be a little suspicious that this is in fact the case, so let us consider another test of the sure-thing principle, this time developed by Allais.[13] Allais' paradox is set out in Figure 12 below.

Your first imaginary choice is to be made between gamble 1 and gamble 2. In gamble 1 you are certain of a payoff of £1,000, whereas in gamble 2 you have a small chance of £5,000, a very good chance of £1,000, but you may not win anything.

Your second choice is between gamble 3 and gamble 4. In gamble 3 you have a small chance of winning £1,000, whereas in gamble 4 you have a slightly worse chance of winning £5,000.

Now, make your choice between gamble 1 and gamble 2 *and* between gamble 3 and gamble 4.

If you have chosen in a way similar to Allais' subjects you will have

Does Subjective Expected Utility Theory Describe Decision-making?

Situation A

	Probability of winning	Amount to win
Gamble 1	100%	£1,000
Gamble 2	10%	£5,000
	89%	£1,000
	1%	Nothing

Situation B

Gamble 3	11%	£1,000
	89%	Nothing
Gamble 4	10%	£5,000
	90%	Nothing

Figure 12. Allais' test of the sure-thing principle

chosen gamble 1 over gamble 2 by reasoning that a certain £1,000 is better than a gamble with the possibility of winning nothing. In your choice between gambles 3 and 4 you may have reasoned that gamble 4 is better than gamble 3 because the probabilities of winning are roughly similar in both gambles and the possible payoff is much larger in gamble 4.

However, as you have probably realized, such a sequence of choices is inconsistent with the sure-thing principle. Now turn to Figure 13, which is an alternative representation of Figure 12.

	Ball numbers		
	1	2–11	12–100
Situation A			
Gamble 1	£1,000	£1,000	£1,000
Gamble 2	Nothing	£5,000	£1,000
Situation B			
Gamble 3	£1,000	£1,000	Nothing
Gamble 4	Nothing	£5,000	Nothing

Figure 13. An alternative representation of Allais' problem

To understand this figure, imagine that the 100 probability points of each gamble have been placed individually on a hundred ping-pong balls. These one hundred balls have been placed in an opaque container and are to be drawn out at random. For example, in gamble 1 if *any* of the numbered balls is drawn out you win £1,000; whereas in gamble 2 if the ball with '1' marked on it is drawn you win nothing. However, if any of the ten balls marked 2 to 11 is drawn you win £5,000. Any one of the eighty-nine remaining balls, those marked 12 to 100, carry a payoff of £1,000.

Now, recall the sure-thing principle which implies that your choices between gambles 1 and 2 and between gambles 3 and 4 are identical! The outcomes not related to your choice, i.e. the payoffs attached to balls 12 to 100 should not affect your choice between the pairs of gambles.

Research on the acceptability of the axioms of SEU has been the subject of much controversy among decision theorists due to its far reaching implications. If your choices were not in accordance with the sure-thing principle then, in a similar manner to our interpretation of the results of showing probability and variance preferences, it follows that SEU is not *descriptive* of your choices amongst simple gambles. However, what would happen if the sure-thing principle were explained to you, without saying it was an axiom of SEU theory, and you were also given *alternative* rationales for choice, such as those I outlined as we worked through the paradoxes, and you were then asked to choose between gambles such as those developed by Ellsberg and Allais? If you rated the alternative rationales as more reasonable or compelling choice principles then the sure-thing principle, this result would have serious implications for the *normative* status of SEU.

Such an empirical study was undertaken by MacCrimmon.[14] He examined the extent to which business executives engaged in a training course for top management positions accepted the sure-thing principle. They were given prepared arguments both conforming with and conflicting with the axiom. The results showed that subjects' initial choices often violated the axioms, and subjects' acceptability ratings of the prepared arguments indicated considerable resistance to the axioms, suggesting that the normative acceptability of SEU was in doubt, at least for these managers. However, during a discussion after the experiment, MacCrimmon found that his managers viewed their choices and ratings as mistakes and so he concluded that the normative status of SEU was not violated.

But Slovic and Tversky[15] questioned MacCrimmon's conclusion. They noted that, whilst MacCrimmon may have been able to get

Does Subjective Expected Utility Theory Describe Decision-making?

the managers to accept the axioms after the discussion, this discussion may not have been neutral. Subtle pressures, together with the undoubted co-operativeness of subjects participating in a training course for top level jobs, may have influenced subjects to conform to axioms outlined by a prestigious decision analyst. Slovic and Tversky asked the question: 'Do reasonable people, who understand the competing arguments, accept the sure-thing principle?' Their results gave a definite 'no' for an answer. Persistent violations of the axiom were found even after it had been explained clearly. Their student subjects tended to prefer alternative choice principles which conflicted with the axiom.

What conclusions can be drawn from the research on the acceptability of the axioms of SEU? First, I think the work on the descriptive relevance of the axioms complements the findings of probability preferences, variance preferences and the dominance of the explicitly stated probabilities and payoffs in determining choice. SEU is clearly not *descriptive* of human choice behaviour in simple choices between gambles. The implication is that this finding will generalize to much more complex real-world decision-making. Second, Slovic and Tversky's results indicate that there is some doubt about the normative status of SEU. By implication, the technology of SEU – decision analysis – is suspect.

However, Slovic and Tversky's paper is but one experiment dealing with one axiom of SEU. More comprehensive experiments must be conducted before SEU is dismissed as the normative theory of decision-making under uncertainty.

Summary

This chapter examined the descriptive relevance of subjective expected utility theory. Research reviewed showed that SEU does not predict choice decisions between simple gambles. Rather, choices seem to be influenced by preferences for various aspects of the gambles such as the probabilities of winning and losing, the amounts to win or lose and their associated distributions. In contrast to the results of this research, preferences between more complex 'duplex' gambles appear to be influenced solely by explicitly presented probabilities and payoffs rather than by their implicit distributions. Nevertheless, the general conclusion from this research is that SEU does not describe choice between gambles and, by generalization, will not describe decision-making under uncertainty in the more complex real-world. This research could, by itself, be taken as prima facie evidence for the necessity to develop and apply decision analysis, the technology of SEU, as a decision aid.

However, other research which has tested the acceptability of a fundamental axiom of SEU, has led to less promising conclusions. The results are currently inconclusive, but they do suggest that there may be some doubt about the normative status of SEU. By implication, decision analysis may be suspect.

4 Individual and Cultural Differences in Decision-making under Uncertainty

This chapter reviews some of my own research on individual and cultural differences in probabilistic thinking. I will describe research relating probabilistic thinking to the personality characteristics of the probability assessor. Next I will recount an investigation of the relative influence of the make-up of the individual decision-maker and the nature of the decision task in the generation of the outcome of a decision.

The second part of this chapter reviews work which has made cross-cultural comparisons on decision-making under uncertainty. Qualitative cultural differences in ways of dealing with uncertainty are shown to be compatible with descriptions of cultural differences in business decision-making.

Questionnaires Used

Almost all the research to be discussed in this chapter has made use of an extended seventy-five question version of the calibration questionnaire similar to that you completed in Chapter 2. In our research Larry Phillips and I called this questionnaire the 'Probability Assessment Questionnaire', or PAQ. We computed several measures from an individual's responses to the PAQ: number of 100 per cent assessments made, number of 50 per cent assessments made, and a measure of the distribution of the seventy-five probability assessments, entropy.[1] The entropy measure is very large when many different assessments are given, and when they are made equally often. The entropy measure would be relatively small for an individual who gave only assessments of 50 per cent and 100 per cent, particularly if most of the assessments were just one of these probabilities. We also computed several mathematical measures of the calibration or realism of the individual's assessed probabilities. These measures summarized the individual's calibration curve. This coding of the PAQ gives an indication both of *numeric* probabilistic set and of calibration.

Another questionnaire that we have used extensively is the 'View of Uncertainty Questionnaire' or VUQ. This questionnaire, which was presented to a subject before the PAQ, asks forty-five questions like: 'Will you catch a head cold in the next three months?' Or, 'Is Baghdad the capital of Iraq?' Half the questions are about events that have not yet happened, while the others concern factual matters that most people are not sure about (e.g. 'Is the Suez Canal over 100 miles long?'). The instructions given at the head of the VUQ are simply to 'Write in the space provided a reasonable and appropriate response to the following questions.' Responses to the VUQ were classified into five categories: number of 'yes/no' responses; number of 'don't know' responses; number of probability responses (e.g. 'very likely', 'improbable', 'perhaps'); number of *different* probability responses used by that individual; and catch-alls (e.g. 'I hope not'). This coding of the VUQ gives an indication of *verbal* probabilistic set.

Individual Comparisons

The literature on authoritarianism, conservatism, dogmatism and intolerence of ambiguity assumes that people who are high scorers on scales measuring these concepts see the world in 'black and white' or, as Souief[2] conceptualizes it, make extreme judgements or responses. As Bochner[3] notes, the primary characteristics of an individual who is intolerant of ambiguity are 'premature closure' and 'need for certainty'. An item from Budner's[4] 'Tolerance–Intolerance of Ambiguity' scale illustrates this: a negative response to 'people who insist on a yes or no answer just don't know how complicated things really are' characterizes a person intolerant of ambiguity. Frenkel-Brunswik, writing in *The Authoritarian Personality*[5] about high F-scale scorers, notes, '. . . a simple, firm, often stereotyped cognitive structure is required. There is no place for ambivalence or ambiguities. Every attempt is made to eliminate them . . .' Rokeach, writing in his book *The Open and Closed Mind*,[6] notes that there is 'relatively little differentiation within the disbelief system' of the high D-scale scoring person. Indeed Ertel[7] has developed a measure of dogmatism based on the content analysis of 'quantifiers' in the publications of writers: dogmatic writers would be expected to use quantifiers such as 'always', 'never', 'nothing but', 'completely', 'must', etc.; whereas non-dogmatic writers would use quantifiers such as 'often', 'rarely', 'greatly', 'considerably', 'can', etc. However, he has not, as yet, linked the content analysis to D-scale scoring.

From these conceptualizations Larry Phillips and I[8] thought that we would obtain strong relationships between these personality variables and measures computed from the VUQ and PAQ. For example, an authoritarian, dogmatic person would perhaps use many 100 per cent responses and be overconfident with these assessments. Conversely, a non-authoritarian, non-dogmatic person would perhaps be more likely to use probabilistic responses to the questionnaires and also be better calibrated than a dogmatic person.

As we expected there to be a wider variation in the responses to our questionnaires in people from the general population, rather than in the more homogeneous student population, we obtained subjects for our experiments by placing newspaper advertisements in local papers. Our results surprised us. They are summarized in Table 1, which is a table of intercorrelations between the personality/cognitive measures and our own measures of probabilistic thinking. A correlation between two variables can range from −1 to +1, with −1 meaning that the two variables are negatively related, i.e. as scores on one variable increase scores on the other variable decrease. In Table 1 the correlation between entropy and number of 100 per cent assessments is −0.48, a result which suggests that people who make fine discriminations of uncertainty use few probability assessments of 100 per cent. This result also suggests the converse: that people who make less fine discriminations of uncertainty tend to use many 100 per cent responses.

A correlation of zero or near zero would suggest that two variables are unrelated. If you look at Table 1 you will see that most of the correlations between the personality/cognitive measures and the probabilistic thinking measures are of this type. A high positive correlation indicates that, as scores on one variable increase, scores on the other variable also increase. Look at the correlations *between* the personality/cognitive variables: they are all positive and fairly high (i.e. above 0.3). This result suggests that authoritarianism, intolerance of ambiguity, conservatism and dogmatism are related personality traits, a result we anticipated from previous personality research.[9]

Only three significant correlations emerged between the two sets of variates. Authoritarianism gave a correlation of −0.41 with percentage correct for 100 per cent assessments, and a correlation of −0.34 with the entropy measure. This result suggests that high-scale scoring

Table 1. Intercorrelation matrix of personality/cognitive measures and probabilistic thinking measures

			A	IT	C	D	YN	DK	PW	DPW	CAL	N 100	PC 100	N50
Personality and cognitive variables	Authoritarianism	(A)												
	Intolerance of ambiguity	(IT)	0.34											
	Conservatism	(C)	0.58											
	Dogmatism	(D)	0.56	0.31	0.38									
Probabilistic thinking variables (verbal)	No. of yes/no	(YN)	0.16	0.06	0.07	0.17								
	No. of don't know	(DK)	−0.26	−0.07	−0.17	−0.29	−0.62							
	No. of probability words	(PW)	−0.06	−0.05	0.01	−0.12	−0.81	0.20						
	No. of different probability words	(DPW)	−0.05	−0.06	−0.08	−0.10	−0.74	0.15	0.87					
Probabilistic thinking variables (numerical)	Calibration	(CAL)	0.06	−0.10	0.01	0.12	−0.07	0.14	0.04	0.08				
	No. of 100 per cent assessments	(N100)	0.20	0.15	0.07	0.23	0.23	−0.27	−0.13	−0.14	−0.07			
	Per cent correct for 100 per cent assessments	(PC100)	−0.41	−0.16	−0.15	−0.19	−0.20	0.16	0.20	0.17	0.05	−0.42		
	No. of 50 per cent assessments	(N50)	0.03	0.06	0.04	−0.08	−0.07	0.25	−0.09	−0.14	0.02	−0.33	−0.05	
	Entropy		−0.34	−0.18	−0.23	−0.21	0.15	0.09	0.17	0.20	0.02	−0.48	0.38	−0.41

authoritarianism is related to poor calibration with 100 per cent assessments, and to a less fine discrimination of probability assessed numerically. Dogmatism gave a correlation of -0.29 with number of don't know responses on the VUQ, suggesting that dogmatic individuals are less likely to say they don't know the answer in uncertain situations.

Apart from these three significant correlations our major conclusion from the study was that an authoritarian, conservative, dogmatic person who is intolerant of ambiguity may be just as capable of probabilistic thinking as is a person of opposite characteristics. A factor analysis of the correlation matrix further revealed that probabilistic thinking itself may be at least a two-factored ability, involving both verbal and numerical processes.

Another important finding from the factor analytic study was that some people, when asked questions about their general knowledge, tend to respond in terms of 'yes', 'no' or 'don't know', while others adopt a 'yes', 'no', 'maybe' view. In other words, one way of viewing may not involve probabilistic processing. This tendency to view the world in terms of certainty or *total* uncertainty we labelled 'non-probabilistic thinking'. The alternative world-view in terms of degrees of probability we labelled 'probabilistic thinking'.

As part of the second stage of our research,[10] we attempted to clarify whether these hypothesized styles of dealing with uncertainty were, indeed, cognitive styles, one of which would characterize a particular individual over a whole range of tasks and situations. If we were able to validate our two alternative cognitive styles over a wide range of tasks involving decision-making under uncertainty then this result could have far-reaching implications for the selection of decision-makers, because probabilistic thinkers, having one prerequisite for an SEU analysis, may be expected to make more optimal decisions than non-probabilistic thinkers.

Before I discuss our findings, let me describe the background to our investigation in a little more detail.

In personality psychology three main theoretical positions describe the individual and his interaction with the environment. Personologism advocates that stable intraorganismic constants such as traits or cognitive styles are the main determinants of behavioural variation (e.g. Alker[11]). Situationism emphasizes environmental (situational) factors as the main sources of behavioural variation (e.g. Mischel[12]). Interactionism, a synthesis of personologism and situationism, implies that the interaction between these two factors is the main source of behavioural variation (e.g. Endler[13]).

One empirical approach to the problem of isolating the sources of behavioural variation has been to use correlational studies employing a sample of individuals, a sample of situations, and a dependent variable that is an indicator of some underlying trait. Given that the measurements of the dependent variable are perfectly reliable, correlation coefficients of unity support personologism. As Ekehammar[14] points out, high correlation coefficients are seldom found and the interactionist view shown by low, but non-zero, correlations is often supported. Zero correlations would favour situationism, provided that there is sufficient variability in response to a situation to allow computation of correlation coefficients and that the dependent variable is adequately represented in each situation. If these conditions are not met, obtained correlations will be attenuated.

Recall that according to the SEU theory of decision-making, optimal choices under uncertainty are made on two independent dimensions of information: probability and utility. As we discussed previously, early research attempted to see if human decision-making could be adequately described by this normative model. Most studies found that, in detail, it could not. Nevertheless, Peterson and Beach concluded:

> 'Experiments that have compared human inferences with those of statistical man show that the normative model provides a good first approximation for a psychological theory of inference. Inferences made by subjects are influenced by appropriate variables in appropriate directions.'[15]

Those studies focusing on the probability dimension have found humans sub-optimal in many ways: for instance, Phillips and Edwards[16] found that people do not extract as much information from probabilistic data as Bayes' theorem[17] would allow; this phenomenon was labelled 'conservatism'. Similarly, as we saw earlier, the general finding from calibration research is overconfidence in probability assessment. In addition, Tversky and Kahneman have outlined heuristics and biases that affect people's judgement of likelihoods in some situations.

Slovic and Hogarth[18] have marshalled this evidence in support of the notion that limited capacity in terms of memory, attention and reasoning capabilities leads the decision-maker to be sub-optimal. Running through these studies is the implicit notion that people think in terms of probability but are not very good at it. As long ago as 1957, Simon,[19] in his theory of 'bounded rationality', has argued that human cognitive limitations often result in poor decision-making.

However, it is not easy to interpret this decision theoretic research as either personologist, situationist or interactionist. As a whole it could be interpreted as supporting any of these positions.

What are the implications for decision-making of our two hypothesized cognitive styles? Are decisions taken differently by probabilistic and non-probabilistic thinkers?

In the second stage of our research we examined the consistency of individual decision-making styles across a much wider variety of tasks than those we used previously.

The tasks utilized in our battery of instruments included: measures of the individual's acceptance of the sure-thing principle; several of Tversky and Kahneman's heuristics; disposition to search for probabilistic (i.e. imperfect, but still useful) information in decision problems; value placed on probabilistic information; and probability revision.

How would a probabilistic thinker with no cognitive limitations perform on these tasks? We expected such a person to accept the axiom of SEU, not to use inappropriate heuristics in judgement of likelihoods, to search for and place value on probabilistic information, and to revise probabilities in accordance with Bayes' theorem. On the other hand, the non-probabilistic thinker translating uncertainty into 'yes/no' or 'don't know' terms would violate the sure-thing principle,[20] tend to use inappropriate heuristics when judging likelihoods, not desire or value probabilistic information, and show poor revision of probabilities in the light of new information.[21]

However, the results of our experiments were contrary to our expectations. We found no high between-task correlations. This result indicated that an individual's performance on a task could not be related to a super-ordinate cognitive style. Similarly, a lack of systematic series of low, but still non-zero, correlations argued against the interactionist's view of decision-making. The evidence seemed to favour situationism. Our results suggested, perhaps rather negatively, that it may well be impossible to select well-rounded decision-makers for decision-making in high-consequence situations. In addition, for any given task, 22 to 88 per cent of our subjects showed little evidence of probabilistic thought. These two findings, taken together, suggest

Behavioral Decision Theory

that task performance is a matter of psychological set rather than of 'bounded rationality' or 'limited capacity' – explanations that are common in the recent literature on behavioural decision theory.

We will return to the interrelationships between situational and personologistic influences on decision-making under uncertainty later. For the moment, note that there is evidence for both individual and task influences on the expression of probabilistic thought. Next, we turn to comparisons between cultures on responses to the VUQ and PAQ.

Cultural Comparisons

Our work on cultural comparisons in decision-making under uncertainty had a starting point in our original work on individual differences. We found that some of the subjects who completed our questionnaires, students at Brunel University, seemed to show little evidence of probabilistic thinking, tending to respond with 50 per cent and 100 per cent assessments to the PAQ and showing poor calibration. On closer investigation we discovered that most of these people came either from Hong Kong or from Malaysia. Was this finding peculiar to South-East Asian students at Brunei?

We decided to make a deeper investigation and, in the first of a series of studies, Fred Ng, Ayleen Wisudha and Irene Tan[22] took the VUQ and PAQ to their home countries of Hong Kong, Indonesia and Malaysia respectively, where several groups of students completed these questionnaires. The calibration results are summarized in Figure 1.

The calibration curves in Figure 1[23] show the British students to be better calibrated in their assessments than the groups of South-East Asian students, who differ little. Whatever numerical assessments the Asian groups gave (except for 100 per cent assessments), they were right roughly 50 per cent of the time. This finding does not bear a simple relationship to the amount of substantive knowledge the groups possess, as there was no sharp distinction between the English and Asian student groups in overall proportion of items answered correctly (British: 0·64; Hong Kong: 0·57; Indonesian: 0·53; Malay Arts: 0·60; and Malay Science students: 0·59).

Other comparisons between the student groups revealed further interesting differences. The British student sample gave the least number of 100 per cent responses to the PAQ (an average of 13, as opposed to Malay Arts: 51; Hong Kong: 25; Indonesian: 37; and Malay

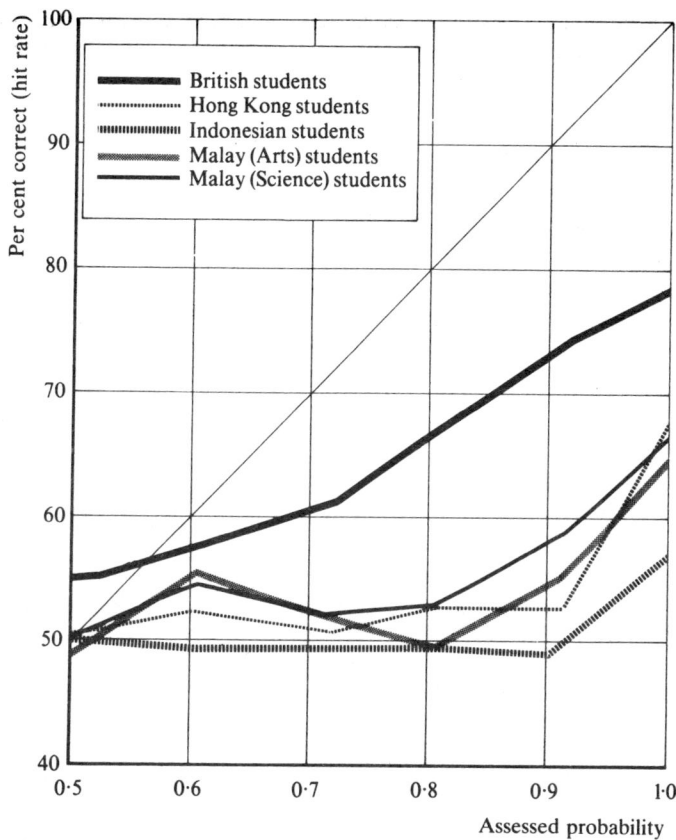

Figure 1. Calibration curves

Science students: 35). Conversely, the British students were best calibrated with these 100 per cent assessments (an average of 84 per cent correct as opposed to the Hong Kong: 70; Indonesian: 58; Malay Arts: 64; and Malay Science students: 67). Similarly, the entropy measure was much higher for the British student sample than for any of the South-East Asian student groups, indicating that the British were expressing a finer differentiation of numerical uncertainty.

Results from the VUQ supported these findings: the British students were found to use many more *different* probability words. We concluded that, at least for student samples studied, South-East Asians show less evidence of probabilistic thinking and more evidence of non-probabilistic thinking than their British counterparts.

Could these results be taken as evidence of a cognitive deficit among South-East Asians? Would our findings generalize to non-students in South-East Asia and Britain? In our next study we attempted to answer these questions.

In our second cross-cultural study[24] we sampled managers in South-East Asia and Britain, reasoning that managers deal with uncertainty as their occupation and so, if cultural differences in probabilistic thinking exist between managers from the cultures studied previously, there is strong evidence for more general cultural influences on decision-making under uncertainty. Figure 2 shows the calibration curves for our samples of managers.

These curves are similar to the calibration curves determined for the student samples: South-East Asian managers show much worse calibration than their British counterparts. The results of cultural comparisons on the other measures taken from the VUQ and PAQ also confirmed our previous result, that people brought up in a South-East Asian culture show little evidence of probabilistic thinking. Asian managers, especially, tended to adopt a 'yes/no' *versus* 'don't know' psychological set for viewing uncertainty, whilst 'yes/no' *versus* a probability assessment was more descriptive of the British managers.

Are cultural differences in probabilistic thinking reflected in management decision-making in the 'real-world' as well as on our questionnaire tasks? Anecdotal evidence seems to confirm the generality of our research findings. For instance, Redding and Martyn-Johns have noted that

'... the commonest of the phrases used by the Western practising manager dealing with his Asian equivalents – "They think differently" ... [and] if probability is seen differently, then this will materially affect the process of management thinking and in turn it will affect management action'.[25]

Non-probabilistic thinking may result in a lack of long-term future planning. Events in the future may be seen as 'uncertain' rather than 'probable' or 'improbable'. For instance, Penny commented about Indonesian agricultural planning:

'Too great a willingness on the part of the government to forgo

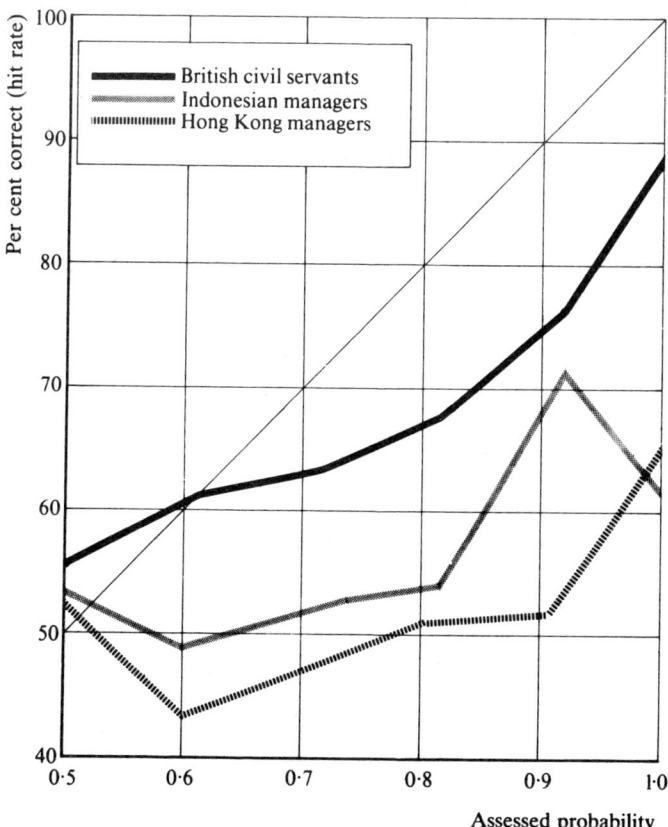

Figure 2. Calibration curves – managerial analysis

future gains for the sake of smaller immediate ones can mean the rejection of extremely profitable development opportunities.'[26]

The successful non-probabilistic thinker, realizing his inability to think probabilistically, may remain flexible in response to an uncertain future. The unsuccessful non-probabilistic thinker may make confident predictions of the future and often be wrong. Conversely, the probabilistic thinker may predict the future in terms of probabilities assigned to events but still be unprepared for actual events, due to lack of perfect calibration.

77

Behavioral Decision Theory

As Redding remarked:

'Why is it that the Chinese form of business is predominantly the small scale, owner-dominated enterprise, with a *reputation for flexibility* and a capacity for survival? ... Instead of surveys of product markets, it relies instead for its strategic thinking on personal recommendations, keeping an ear to the ground, having a highly developed sense of the complete context in which it operates, and *following hunches*. It takes risks but not based on probability theory ... It goes without saying the Chinese have a flair for business. It also seems evident that their managerial methods are not the same as are found in a Western company. The contrast seems to be between the Western sense of order and rationality and the Oriental sense of all-embracing contextual thinking in which the *options are always open, the view can change* and sense or feel takes over from calculation. It is arts versus science.'[27]

I believe that it is clear from this analysis that probabilistic and non-probabilistic thinking may be qualitatively different ways of dealing with uncertainty, at least in calibration studies. Our findings do not imply cultural deficit. Indeed, in an age of rapid and unpredictable change the non-probabilistic thinker may be at an advantage over the probabilistic thinker. Consider an example of the failure of a probabilistic decision analysis undertaken by Watson and Brown[28] and reported in Humphreys.[29] Watson and Brown recounted the results of a decision analysis facing the Neer[30] motor company in 1972. Neer's parts division wanted to decide whether or not to become involved in car tyres. Humphreys succinctly summarizes Neer's options:

'Neer had to choose between four immediate acts: (i) *do nothing*, (ii) accept a *deal* with a major tyre manufacturer to supply their product at a discount, (iii) investigate the possibility of Neer producing its own *private brand* of tyre, (iv) *wait about 3 years* before making a decision. Neer considered the key uncertain events to be (i) whether or not Trimark Motors[31] (a major competitor) would decide to make their own brand of tyre, (ii) whether the government would exert pressure on motor manufacturers to include tyres in their warranties, and (iii) what the increased cost to Neer of using private branded tyres would be.'

As you will have appreciated, the problem was quite complex, with many act and event linkages represented in the form of a 'bushy' decision tree. The result of the decision analysis prescribed that Neer should investigate private branding immediately, which it did. However, as it turned out, the decision analysis was what Humphreys calls a 'fantasy of the future'. It turned out that not *one* tyre manufacturer was willing to bid for Neer's contract, and Neer were forced to choose the act that they would have anyway if no decision analysis had been performed: wait for three years. In this example the consequences of an inappropriate representation of the decision problem facing Neer were not catastrophic, but it is not hard to imagine decision situations where inappropriate problem representation may have more serious consequences. To re-quote Fischhoff:

> '... Decision Analysis is orientated to picking the apparent best alternative rather than to assessing the adequacy of our knowledge, it may encourage us to act where ignorance dictates hesitation or continued information gathering.'[32]

Summary

This chapter reviewed research in individual and cultural differences in probabilistic thinking. Probabilistic thinking appears not to be strongly related to the personality/cognitive measures of authoritarianism, dogmatism, conservatism and intolerance of ambiguity. However, there is some evidence that high scale scoring authoritarianism is related to poor calibration with certainty responses and to less fine discrimination of probability expressed numerically. Furthermore, dogmatic individuals are less likely to say they don't know in uncertain situations.

Results of a factor analytic study of this data indicated that some individuals may be non-probabilistic thinkers, tending to see the world in terms of certainty or total uncertainty. An alternative world-view, identified as a differentiation of uncertainty in terms of degrees of probability, we labelled probabilistic thinking. However, investigation of the generality of these alternative cognitive styles over a wider range of tasks involving decision-making under uncertainty revealed that task influences on performance were more important.

Cultural comparisons on calibration and related measures of probabilistic thinking revealed strong cultural differences between students and managers from Britain, and those from Hong Kong, Indonesia and Malaysia. Generally, Asians were found to adopt a less finely differentiated view of uncertainty both numerically and verbally than did

Behavioral Decision Theory

a British sample. Numerical probabilities assessed by the Asians were more extreme and less realistic than those assessed by the British sample. It was argued that there are qualitative cultural differences in ways of dealing with uncertainty on these tasks. The relative success of the two alternative ways of dealing with uncertainty depends on the prevailing external environmental conditions.

5 Revision of Opinion

This chapter deals with theory and research on human revision of opinion. As we saw in Chapter 1, subjective probability is a measure of our opinion about the likelihood of an event. In Chapter 2 we dealt with the calibration of subjective probabilities, where subjective probability was used as a representation of our degree of belief in the truth of a statement or proposition.

Next we turn to the topic of changes in opinion, or subjective probability, in the light of new information.

Your Decision Problem

Imagine that you are the gunnery officer on board a naval destroyer at war with a foreign power. An unidentified plane shows upon the edge of the radar screen of one of your ratings. You know that both friendly and enemy planes are in the general area of your ship and reason that, since an enemy plane is unlikely to launch an attack by itself, your *prior opinion* that the plane is hostile is fairly low. However, as the plane draws nearer your ship it fails to respond to radio messages and will not identify itself. In the light of this *likelihood information* your initially low prior opinion that the plane is an enemy increases somewhat, but not greatly, because you know that the radio transceivers on some types of friendly aircraft are particularly prone to damage. A visual sighting of the aircraft from your ship shows the plane to be a similar type to a common allied plane, so you revise your opinion that the plane is unfriendly downward, and thus increase your opinion that the plane is friendly. However, you realize that some of the newest enemy jets are thought to be very similar to some of the allied planes. The jet continues on a flight path towards your own ship. Soon you will be within its rocket range. Fighter aircraft sent from an aircraft carrier in your convoy reach the unidentified plane and engage in an aerial combat with it. Your *posterior opinion* is now near certainty that the suspect aircraft is unfriendly and you instruct your gunners to open fire.

This imaginary decision problem illustrates *intuitive* revision of opinion in the light of information received. Intuitive opinion revision may, or may not, make best use of the information available to the decision-maker.

As we saw earlier, SEU theory can be shown to be a normative theory of decision-making under uncertainty, if you accept the underlying axioms. However, SEU is a static theory of choice, in that the probabilities required as inputs are single unique estimates. *Bayes' theorem*, by contrast, is a dynamic theory of normative opinion revision used for updating prior opinion, or initial probabilities, as more information is received. Like SEU theory, Bayes' theorem is a normative theory derived from certain fundamental axioms or first principles. If you, as the decision-maker, accept the axioms then it can be shown that *if* your intuitive opinion revision and that prescribed by Bayes' theorem conflict, your opinions will be more valid if they follow the updating specified by the theorem. I will now outline the axioms of Bayes' theorem.

AXIOMS OF BAYES' THEOREM

1. 'A probability is a number which lies between zero and one, and the probability of a sure event is one.'
2. 'The sum of the probabilities of an exhaustive set of mutually exclusive events is equal to one.'

    For example, a dice has six sides, so the probability of a specified single side landing face up when I throw a 'fair' dice is $\frac{1}{6} + \frac{1}{6} + \frac{1}{6} + \frac{1}{6} + \frac{1}{6} + \frac{1}{6} = 1$. In other words I am certain that one side of the dice will land face-up.
3. 'The probability of either of two mutually exclusive events occurring is equal to the sum of their individual probabilities.'

    For example, a dice has six sides, so the probability of *either* a two or a three landing face-up is $\frac{1}{6} + \frac{1}{6} = \frac{1}{3}$. In the case of a toss of a coin the probability of *either* heads or tails landing face up is $\frac{1}{2} + \frac{1}{2} = 1$, or certainty.
4. 'The probability of *both* event A and event B occurring is equal to the probability of event A multiplied by the probability of event B *given* that event A has occurred.'

Revision of Opinion

For example, consider the possible outcome of two throws of a coin shown in Figure 1. In this case the probability of a head on the second throw *given* that a tail has been thrown on the first throw is $\frac{1}{2}$ (remember, the coin has no memory!) because the events are *independent*. However, consider the probability of drawing two

Probability of two heads:	$H\,H = \frac{1}{2} \times \frac{1}{2} = \frac{1}{4}$
Probability of two tails:	$T\,T = \frac{1}{2} \times \frac{1}{2} = \frac{1}{4}$
Probability of a head then a tail:	$H\,T = \frac{1}{2} \times \frac{1}{2} = \frac{1}{4}$
Probability of a tail then a head:	$T\,H = \frac{1}{2} \times \frac{1}{2} = \frac{1}{4}$
	Sum = 1

Figure 1. An illustration of the fourth axiom of Bayes' theorem.

consecutive aces from a pack of fifty-two playing cards *without* replacing the first card drawn back into the pack of cards. The probability of drawing an ace on the first draw is $\frac{4}{52}$ because there are four aces in the pack of fifty-two cards. However, if the first card drawn is an ace there are now three aces left amongst the remaining fifty-one cards. So the probability of drawing an ace the second time is $\frac{3}{51}$ *given* that an ace has been drawn the first time. The two events are not independent of each other. Conversely, if an ace was not drawn the first time, the chances of drawing an ace the second time are slightly increased, to $\frac{4}{51}$. The probability of drawing two consecutive aces is $\frac{4}{52} \times \frac{3}{51} = \frac{12}{2652}$, or about a 0·005 probability!

From the four basic axioms it is possible to derive Bayes' theorem. There are several algebraic versions of Bayes' theorem, some of which are more complicated than others. In its simplest form Bayes' theorem states that your posterior opinion that a hypothesis is true is the product of your prior opinion multiplied by the likelihood of the obtained data, or information, *given* that the hypothesis is true.

To illustrate Bayes' theorem, consider the following example. Imagine that I have two opaque book-bags[1] each containing one hundred poker-chips. One of the bags, bag A, contains seventy blue poker-chips and thirty red poker-chips, while the other bag, bag B, contains seventy red poker-chips and thirty blue poker-chips – exactly the opposite! I am now going to place the two bags behind my back and then choose one of the bags at random and place it in front of me. Next I will dip my hand into the opaque bag, shuffle the poker-chips, and pull one out and show you its colour. I will then replace it in the

83

Behavioral Decision Theory

bag with the other poker-chips, re-shuffle them, and pull out another poker-chip for you to see.

Both poker-chips were coloured blue. What is your posterior opinion that the bag I initially chose was bag A? What is your posterior opinion that the bag was bag B?

Let's see how Bayes' theorem would solve this problem. Table 1 shows how 50–50 prior opinion was changed to posterior opinion of 35–15 in favour of bag B on a sample of *one* blue poker-chip.

In this simple form of Bayes' theorem the sum of the products of priors multiplied by likelihoods for the two hypotheses under consideration is less than one. To convert these odds of 35 to 15 (or 7 to 3) to probabilities you should divide the product of 'prior × likelihood' for each hypothesis by this sum, as shown in Table 1.

Table 1. Revision of opinion performed by Bayes' theorem after the first draw from the bag

Hypotheses	Prior opinion	Likelihoods	Priors × likelihoods	Posterior opinion
Bag A	0·5	0·7	0·35	$\frac{0·35}{0·50} = 0·7$
Bag B	0·5	0·3	0·15	$\frac{0·15}{0·50} = 0·3$
			Sum = 0·50	Sum = 1·0

So, after seeing one blue poker-chip drawn from the bag, your prior opinion that the bag I have chosen is bag A has changed from 0·5 to a posterior opinion of 0·7. Conversely, your posterior opinion that I have chosen bag B is now 0·3.

These posterior opinions are now your prior opinions *before* you see the result of my second draw from the bag. The revision of opinion caused by a second blue poker-chip being drawn is shown in Table 2.

After two blue poker-chips Bayes' theorem states that you should assess a 0·84 probability that the chosen bag is bag A and a 0·16 probability that the chosen bag is bag B.

Revision of Opinion

Table 2. Revision of opinion performed by Bayes' theorem after the second draw from the bag

Hypotheses	Prior opinion	Likelihoods	Priors × likelihoods	Posterior opinion
Bag A	0·7	0·7	0·49	$\frac{0·49}{0·58} = 0·84$
Bag B	0·3	0·3	0·09	$\frac{0·09}{0·58} = 0·16$
			Sum = 0·58	Sum = 1·00

Does Bayes' Theorem Describe Your Opinion Revision?

To answer this question I'd like you to take part in a probability revision task similar to the example I have just given you.

Imagine that you are shown three opaque cloth bags. One contains seventy black marbles and thirty white marbles. We will call this bag B, for it is predominantly black. The second bag contains fifty black marbles and fifty white marbles. We will call this bag Q. The third bag contains forty black marbles and sixty white marbles. We will call this bag W, for it is predominantly white. The bags are illustrated in Figure 2.

Figure 2. The three opaque cloth bags

Imagine that one of the three bags has been chosen at random. Now, which bag do you think is more likely to be the chosen bag? Circle your answer (circle all three if you think the bags are equally likely).

Bag B   Bag Q   Bag W

Behavioral Decision Theory

You should have circled all three because choosing one of them randomly ensured that each was equally likely to have been chosen.

The following problems *start* with the assumption that the bags are equally likely to have been chosen, so keep this in mind.

For each problem, marbles will be randomly drawn out of a single bag, one at a time. After each marble is shown to you, it is returned to the bag and the contents are mixed before the next marble is randomly drawn. Your job after each draw is to decide which bag is more likely and then to circle your choice on Figure 3. Then, carefully estimate how much more likely that bag is to be the chosen one rather than the other two. You do this by distributing your probabilities between the bags as follows:

Perhaps you think that bag W is most likely to be the chosen bag so you circle bag W.

The chosen bag is:

Bag B	Bag Q	(Bag W)

How much more likely?

Bag B	Bag Q	(Bag W)
0·1	0·2	0·7

By putting 0·7 under bag W you are saying that you think that there is a 0·7 probability that it is bag W, a 0·2 probability it is bag Q and a 0·1 probability it is bag B. (NB: Check that the sum of the probabilities you give always is 1·0.)

To summarize, you will be shown a sequence of draws all made from *either* bag R, bag Q or bag W. You will see one marble at a time. After you have seen a marble you will first state which bag is more likely to have been the chosen bag, the bag from which the marbles are being drawn, and then you will estimate how much more likely. You will then see the next marble to be drawn from the bag.

Now turn to Figure 3. Please consider each draw separately and try not to look at the results of the next draw until you have completed your response to the preceding draw.

Now turn to Appendix 2 (p. 117). This contains the posterior opinions as calculated by Bayes' theorem. Do your posterior opinions

Revision of Opinion

Draw 1	○	Bag B	Bag Q	Bag W
Draw 2	○	Bag B	Bag Q	Bag W
Draw 3	●	Bag B	Bag Q	Bag W
Draw 4	●	Bag B	Bag Q	Bag W
Draw 5	○	Bag B	Bag Q	Bag W
Draw 6	○	Bag B	Bag Q	Bag W
Draw 7	●	Bag B	Bag Q	Bag W
Draw 8	●	Bag B	Bag Q	Bag W
Draw 9	○	Bag B	Bag Q	Bag W
Draw 10	●	Bag B	Bag Q	Bag W

Figure 3. The result of draws from the bags shown in Figure 2

match? In Appendix 2 the highest degree of posterior opinion attached to the bag most favoured by Bayes' theorem after each draw is boxed.

Next I'd like you to calculate how much your opinion revision differs from that specified by Bayes' theorem. For each of the ten draws, examine the posterior opinion attached to the bag *most favoured* by Bayes' theorem. For draw one the bag is bag W, and Bayes' theorem has placed a 0·43 probability on this bag. Now take the probability you assessed from that given by Bayes' theorem. For instance, if the probability you gave was 0·30 the answer would be 0·13. Conversely, if you assessed 0·50 then the answer would be −0·07. Finally add together the answers or, more formally, the *signed deviations*, for the ten draws.

You'll probably find that your signed deviation is quite high and positive. In other words your posterior opinion was not as extreme as that calculated by Bayes' theorem. This result has been termed 'conservatism'. It has been a general finding that in these sorts of tasks people do not extract as much information from the data as the normative theory would allow. In other words posterior probabilities assessed intuitively tend to be closer to the corresponding prior probabilities than are the posterior probabilities calculated via Bayes' theorem. So, Bayes' theorem does not *describe* human revision of probability. This finding is analogous to the finding that SEU does not describe decision-making under uncertainty. Research that has investigated the limitations of human probability revision will be presented in more detail later in this chapter.

Is Bayes's theorem a *normative* theory of opinion revision? Do people, in general, accept the axioms of the theorem? I know of no research on the acceptability of the first axiom.[2] Research on the descriptive relevance of the second axiom has been meagre and contradictory. For instance, Phillips *et al.*,[3] in a probability revision task, found four out of their five subjects assessed probabilities that were greater than unity. These four subjects increased their probability estimates for likely hypotheses but failed to decrease probabilities attached to unlikely hypotheses. In another probability revision study Marks and Clarkson[4] found that forty-nine out of their sixty-two subjects gave probability estimates for complementary events that summed to more than unity. Conversely, a study of Alberoni,[5] which asked subjects to estimate sampling distributions from binominal populations on the basis of small samples, found that in most cases subjective probabilities summed to less than unity.

Non-conformity to the second axiom can be overcome by having the probability assessor divide a line into n segments, each one proportional by length to one of the n events' probabilities. Such a procedure would be justifiable *if* the probability assessor accepted the normative status of the axiom.

Studies of the descriptive relevance of the third and fourth axioms are fairly positive. Barclay and Beach[6] found that the third axiom best described their subjects' assessments, although there was some tendency to underestimate these probabilities. Research on the fourth axiom is contradictory. Peterson *et al.*[7] found close approximation of the axiom to related assessments, while Barclay and Beach[8] found that subjects tended to slightly overestimate the probabilities involved.

Clearly, in contrast to the research with the axioms of SEU theory, the axioms of Bayes' theorem have a good degree of descriptive validity. No one has attempted to assess their normative acceptability, as Slovic and Tversky did with the axioms of SEU, perhaps because the axioms of Bayes' theorem seem intuitively more reasonable.

Studies of Human Opinion Revision

How well does Bayes' theorem, the theorem derived from the axioms, *describe* human opinion revision? The data from a large number of laboratory studies, using tasks very similar to the one you have just completed, shows that the amount of opinion revision is often less than the theorem would prescribe. However, the *amount* of 'conservatism' shown in a particular task is highly situation specific.

The degree of conservatism has been shown to vary with the *diagnosticity* of the data. For example, imagine that you were being shown samples drawn from one of two opaque bags each containing a hundred coloured balls. One of the bags contains forty-nine red balls and fifty-one blue balls, while the other contains fifty-one red and forty-nine blue. Clearly, two consecutive samples each of a blue ball would not be very diagnostic as to which bag was generating the data. Experiments have shown that the more diagnostic the data the less optimal the subject. When the data becomes very undiagnostic, as in the above example, human probability revision can become too extreme.

Another variable which affects the amount of conservatism exhibited is the way in which data is presented. According to Bayes' theorem it should not matter whether a series of data is presented sequentially or all at once. However, Peterson et al.[9] found that subjects' estimates were less conservative when a sample of data was presented one item at a time, with probability revisions required after each item, than they were when they made a single estimate of their posterior probabilities based on the information contained in the whole sample. A further finding is that, even when data is presented sequentially, the *ordering* or sequence of the data influences probability revision. Pitz, Downing and Reinhold[10] described an 'inertia effect', where subjects tended *not* to revise their probabilities downward once the *initial* part of a sequence of data had favoured one of the hypotheses under consideration. In other words, subjects seemed unwilling to reduce their probabilities on a favoured hypothesis following disconfirming evidence.

DuCharme and Peterson[11] investigated human probability revision in a situation they considered to be nearer to real life than the bookbag and poker-chip paradigm. They argued that the datum in the latter paradigm is usually restricted to one of two different types, e.g. a red or a blue poker-chip, and that there are usually only two or three possible revisions that can be made on the information obtained. In real life, information may vary along a continuum rather than being discrete values. In their study, DuCharme and Peterson used a hypothesis set consisting of the population of male heights and the population of female heights. The subjects' task was to decide which population was being sampled on the basis of the data contained in randomly sampled heights from that population. Using this task, DuCharme and Peterson found conservatism *half as great* as with the typical book-bag and poker-chip task. They concluded that this effect was due to their subjects' greater familiarity with the data generating process underlying their task.

Winkler and Murphy[12] took DuCharme's arguments one stage further. In an article entitled 'Experiments in the laboratory and the real world' they argued that, even though the typical book-bag and poker-chip paradigm seems outwardly simple, it differs in four major respects from the real world.

First, the inference tasks so far discussed differ from everyday situations in that, in most of the laboratory tasks, samples of data are *conditionally independent*. That is, two or more pieces of information have an *identical* implication for the posterior opinion to be placed on a particular hypothesis no matter if the pieces of information are considered jointly or in *any* sequence. In the real world, Winkler and Murphy argue, successive items of information may be, to a degree, redundant. This would mean that the total impact of several pieces of information would be less than the sum of the impacts of each item, *assuming* the other data had not been observed. To quote Winkler and Murphy:

> 'Therefore, one possible explanation for conservatism in simple book-bag and poker-chip experiments is that the subject is behaving as he does in more familiar situations involving redundant information sources' (p. 256).

Second, in most experiments using the book-bag and poker-chip paradigm the data generators (the book-bags) are *stationary*. That is, the contents of the book-bag remain the same during the experiment. In the real world our hypotheses may not remain constant. Indeed, the nature of information obtained may change our hypotheses.

Third, in the real world data may be *unreliable* and therefore be less diagnostic than perfectly reliable data, like the colour of a poker-chip. For example, unreliable data may come from an untrained plane-spotter in the example given at the beginning of this chapter. In many real-life opinion revisions the probability assessor not only has to determine the diagnosticity of a piece of data but also its reliability.[13] In support of Winkler and Murphy's argument Youssef and Peterson[14] have shown that, when laboratory tasks include unreliable data, human inference tends to be less conservative, but still not in accordance with Bayes' theorem.

Fourth, subjects in the book-bag and poker-chip experiment are typically given highly diagnostic data. In the real world, data may be relatively *undiagnostic* and so the result of subjects generalizing their experience of the real world to the novel laboratory task may result in conservatism.

In summary, Winkler and Murphy conclude that 'conservatism may be an artifact caused by dissimilarities between the laboratory and the real world'. However, despite these criticisms of the results of laboratory experiments, there has been a considerable research effort into the development of computer-aided Probabilistic Information Processing Systems (PIP Systems) that implement Bayes' theorem. In these systems, the probability assessor makes the probability judgement after each item of information arrives, but the computer *aggregates* these assessments. Of course, it is usually impossible in real life to check the veracity of prior opinion, likelihoods and posterior opinion against a suitable agreed-upon criterion, as it is in laboratory investigations of opinion revision. This fact accounts for the rarity of studies of opinion revision in the real world that are analogous to those studied so intensively in the laboratory. Why then should PIP Systems be implemented as decision aids? The credibility of PIP Systems rests on a seminal series of studies conducted by Ward Edwards and his colleagues.

Probabilistic Information Processing Systems

Edwards, Phillips, Hayes and Goodman[15] investigated probability revision in a simulation study of political-military decision-making. Edwards *et al.* trained their subjects in the history of the world in the then-future – 1975. In 1975 the world was supposedly made up of six major nations. Subjects were given six hypotheses about the state of the world (e.g. 'Russia is about to attack the United Arab Republic') and were asked to make probabilistic inferences about these hypotheses on the basis of information from surveillance satellites, radar and reports from intelligence experts. Each subject was given sixty pieces of sequential information.

The subjects were divided into groups. Some were required to assess likelihoods in the form of likelihood ratios after each datum (called the PIP condition), while others were simply asked to assess the final posterior probabilities, or odds, for the hypotheses under consideration (unaided inference conditions).

Edwards *et al.*'s results indicated that both the PIP condition and the unaided inference conditions favoured the same hypothesis after the sixty items of data had been evaluated. The PIP System was superior to unaided inference in that it favoured the hypothesis that was eventually agreed upon *much earlier* in the data sequence. In other words the PIP System extracted much more certainty from the data. However, Kaplan and Newman[16] found that PIP Systems were inferior to ideal performance, shown when Bayes' theorem was used to aggregate *objective* priors and likelihoods compared to the use of Bayes' theorem to aggregate *subjective* priors and likelihoods. Nevertheless, in their series of experiments PIP was superior to the unaided inference conditions, where subjects were simply asked to assess a single posterior opinion about the likelihood of a particular hypothesis given the sequence of data. This result suggests that the causes of conservatism include the *misaggregation* of prior opinion and likelihoods *and* the *misperception* of the diagnosticity of individual datum.

Overall, the evidence favours the use of PIP Systems over unaided posterior assessment. However, it must be emphasized that the simulation studies cited above have exclusively used independent data rather than dependent data. Domas and Peterson[17] have suggested that if dependent data is to be used as the basis for opinion revision then it should itself be aggregated into data groupings which are independent from one another. Likelihoods and likelihood ratios for these data groupings could then be assessed in the normal way for input to a PIP System. However, it may, of course, be difficult to determine whether or not conditional dependencies exist among the data.

To summarize, a PIP System is, simply, the multiplication of prior probabilities by likelihoods, as they are input by the probability assessor, and then additions and a long division are performed to compute posterior probabilities. These posterior probabilities are then used as the new prior probabilities to be combined with new likelihoods as new information arrives. As you would expect, computers are often used to automate the aggregation of judgements required by Bayes' theorem. Interest in PIP systems has been especially noticeable in the area of military decision-making. However, as perhaps you might anticipate, the procedures used are usually classified and therefore

Revision of Opinion

unavailable. For this reason, and also to provide a means of contrast, I will now discuss the issue of probabilistic information processing in a clinical setting.

Revision of Opinion in a Clinical Setting

Graham and Kendall's[18] Memory-for-Designs Test has been used to diagnose brain damage. Graham and Kendall found that 50 per cent of brain damaged people scored above a criterion level, while 4 per cent of people who were functionally ill scored above this level.

Imagine that a psychiatrist makes a preliminary diagnosis of a patient as either functionally ill *or* brain damaged. After a preliminary investigation he is about equally sure of either diagnosis. He then gives the Memory-for-Designs Test to the patient and the patient scores above the criterion level. How sure should the psychiatrist now be about each of the two possible diagnoses?[19]

Table 3. Calculation of posterior opinion with 50–50 prior opinion

Hypotheses	Priors	Likelihoods	Priors × likelihoods	Posteriors
Functional illness	0·5	0·04	0·02	$\frac{0·02}{0·27} = 0·07$
Brain damage	0·5	0·50	0·25	$\frac{0·25}{0·27} = 0·93$
			Sum = 0·27	Sum = 1·00

Bayes' theorem states that our prior opinion multiplied by our likelihood gives us our posterior opinion. Table 3 sets out the calculations with 50–50 prior opinion. In this example posterior odds have been converted to posterior probabilities.

Therefore, after seeing the test result the psychiatrist is 7 per cent sure the patient is functionally ill and 93 per cent sure of brain damage. Prior uncertainty of 0·5–0·5 has changed to posterior uncertainty of 0·07–0·93.

Suppose the psychiatrist consulted the records of the hospital to provide a basis for assessing these prior probabilities and that he discovered that only 20 per cent of the patients at the hospital in the past

Behavioral Decision Theory

have been functionally ill, and that 80 per cent were brain damaged. Next, suppose he used these figures as his prior probabilities. Let's see what effect this change in prior opinion has on his posterior opinion. Table 4 sets out the calculations.

Table 4. Calculation of posterior opinion with 80–20 prior opinion

Hypotheses	Priors	Likelihoods	Priors × likelihoods	Posteriors
Functional illness	0·2	0·04	0·01	$\frac{0·01}{0·41} = 0·02$
Brain damage	0·8	0·50	0·40	$\frac{0·40}{0·41} = 0·98$
			Sum = 0·41	Sum = 1·00

After seeing exactly the same test result the psychiatrist is 2 per cent sure the patient is functionally ill and 98 per cent sure of brain damage. The test, patient and psychiatrist are identical in the calculations of Tables 3 and 4; only the prior opinion has changed.

Next consider the case where the patient does *not* score above the criterion level. The appropriate calculations are given in Table 5.

Table 5. Calculation of posterior opinion where the patient does not score above the criterion level

Hypotheses	Priors	Likelihoods	Priors × likelihoods	Posteriors
Functional illness	0·2	0·96	0·19	$\frac{0·19}{0·59} = 0.32$
Brain damage	0·8	0·50	0.40	$\frac{0·40}{0·59} = 0·68$
			Sum = 0·59	Sum = 1·00

This time prior probabilities of 0·2–0·8 have changed to posteriors of 0·32–0·68. It is important to notice that the psychiatrist's posterior probabilities still favour the diagnosis 'brain damage' even though the patient did not show a score indicating brain damage. The Bayesian psychiatrist would conclude that the test would not change his prior probabilities enough to warrant its use.

Other important points to note are that prior opinions and likelihoods need not be based on 'actuarial' or relative frequency data as they are in this example. Bayes' theorem applies equally well to the revision of subjective probabilities in the light of new information. This fact is especially useful where base-rate data is non-existent or believed to be unreliable.

In a medical setting, Diamond and Forrester[20] note that the diagnosis of coronary heart disease has become increasingly complex. Many different results obtained from diagnostic tests with substantial imperfections must be integrated into a diagnostic conclusion about the probability of coronary-artery disease in a given patient. These authors collected data on the pre-test likelihood of the disease (defined by age, sex and symptoms) and the sensitivity and specificity of four diagnostic tests: stress electro-cardiography, cardiokymography, thallium scintigraphy and cardiac fluoroscopy. With this information, test results of an individual patient can be analysed by use of Bayes' theorem. The authors point out the advantages of this approach and state that it may assist in decisions on cost-effectiveness of diagnostic tests.

Computers have been used to perform the tedious calculations of posterior probabilities in medical diagnosis with the clinician and/or actuarial tables inputting prior opinion and likelihoods. Uses include diagnosis of thyroid disease, causes of acute renal failure and paternity evaluation.[21]

In practical terms one use of Bayes' theorem is to decide when test administration is unnecessary because the weight of prior opinion will remain unchanged whatever the test result. Another use is to stop the administration of diagnostic tests when a threshold probability level, e.g. 95 per cent sure of a diagnosis, is reached.

Summary

This chapter introduced Bayes' theorem as a normative theory of opinion revision in the light of new information. The normative status of Bayes' theorem is, in a similar manner to SEU, based on the acceptance of fundamental axioms. In contrast to SEU, the axioms of Bayes' theorem are relatively uncontroversial and so the normative status of the theorem is fairly safe. However, Bayes' theorem was

Behavioral Decision Theory

shown to be a poor descriptor of human revision of opinion in laboratory tasks. Several explanations of the 'sub-optimal' performance of human decision-makers were discussed and computer based systems which implement Bayes' theorem in order to aid human judgement were described. Examples of the use of Bayes' theorem in clinical decision problems were given.

6 Descriptive Theories of Decision-making

This chapter presents a discussion of the 'state of the art' in descriptive decision theory research. Whereas the research discussed in the previous chapters is essentially pre-theoretical, having documented the descriptive shortcomings of the normative models of decision-making, later studies have attempted to provide descriptions of the psychological processes underlying observed decision behaviour.

Decision-making under Uncertainty

As we have seen in earlier chapters, SEU does not describe decision-making under uncertainty, even in the context of choices between simple gambles. Other theories have been developed to describe this decision-making. Slovic and Lichtenstein,[1] using the duplex gambles described in Chapter 3 and a regression procedure utilizing the four 'basic' risk dimensions involved in the gambles (amount to win (W); amount to lose (L); probability of winning (PW); and probability of losing (PL)), found that a simple 'additive model' could account for rated attractiveness of a gamble. The model proposed by Slovic and Lichtenstein is:

$$\text{Attractiveness} = \mu + W_1 PW + W_2 \$W + W_3 PL + W_4 \$L$$

In the model μ is a scaling constant. Slovic and Lichtenstein had their subjects rate the attractiveness of many gambles. As the values of the four 'risk' dimensions for each of the gambles were known, it was possible for Slovic and Lichtenstein to estimate, using the regression procedure, the relative contributions of the four risk dimensions to the attractiveness ratings of the gambles for a particular subject. Slovic and Lichtenstein found that this model correlated 0·86, on average, with the attractiveness of a gamble when attractiveness was determined either by a selling price procedure or a rating procedure.[2] On average,

Behavioral Decision Theory

PW made the highest contribution to attractiveness when this was determined by subjective ratings, while the monetary payoffs contributed most to attractiveness when this was shown by the setting of selling prices for the gambles.

This additive model is, of course, in complete contrast to the SEU theory, which involves addition and *multiplication* to evaluate the attractiveness of a gamble. However, the model proposed by Slovic and Lichtenstein is not without its critics. Shanteau[3] argued that correlations do not by themselves provide an adequate index of the 'goodness of fit' of the model to the data. Using analysis of variance techniques Shanteau re-analysed Slovic and Lichtenstein's original data and was able to show evidence for probability-by-payoff interactions which are contrary to the additive model but are in accordance with multiplicative theories like SEU. Clearly, the additive model does not provide a total description of human evaluation of duplex gambles.

Shanteau[4] has developed his own 'Information-Integration' approach to a description of decision-making under uncertainty where:

$$R = \Sigma W_i S_i$$

Here R refers to subjects' response on a numerical scale, S_i is the subjective value of an outcome, and W_i is the subjective likelihood of getting outcome S_i.

For evaluation of a simple two-outcome gamble, information integration theory can be rewritten as:

$$R = W_1 S_1 + W_2 S_2$$

This implies a multiplying model for each part of the bet and an adding model for the combination of the two parts. As you will have realized, information integration theory and SEU appear to be very similar approaches. However, as Shanteau points out, the two approaches have different derivations:

> 'The SEU approach is derived from economic theory and includes normative elements related to maximization of utility. In contrast the integration approach is based on psychological theory and is fundamentally descriptive. The goal of this approach has been to develop an empirical foundation for descriptive laws of behaviour.

Another view of the difference between SEU and integration theories can be seen in the interpretation of the parameters. For instance, the concept of weight in integration theory is more general

Descriptive Theories of Decision-making

than the concept of subjective probability in SEU theory. Thus, a chance of losing might be given more weight than an equivalent chance of winning. Similarly, scale value reflects more than utility, so that a crisp dollar bill might be valued more than a crumpled one. At the level of parameters, therefore, integration theory provides a more general approach' (pp. 133–4).[5]

In addition, unlike SEU, the weights in the integration model do not have to sum to one. Using simple gambles, Anderson and Shanteau[6] and Shanteau[7] claim some empirical support for the theory. But a crucial experiment to decide the descriptive dominance of either integration theory or SEU has, to my mind, not yet been conducted. To quote Shanteau, 'As far as the present data are concerned, the SEU and integration models share a similar fate.'

Another approach to deriving descriptions of decision-making under uncertainty has been developed by Clyde Coombs and his associates in his 'Portfolio Theory of Risk', which makes use of the concepts of risk and risk preference. As we saw in Chapter 2, the notion of risk is incorporated into SEU by way of the shape of a person's utility function for money. By itself, risk does not play a major role in SEU. By contrast, Coombs has argued that choices amongst gambles are determined *in part* by maximizing expected value and *in part* by the individual *optimizing his or her preferred level of risk*. In one early experiment, Coombs and Meyer[8] studied how people ranked ordered two-outcome gambles in relation to their perceived 'riskiness'. They held expected value constant by using the imaginary paradigm of a coin

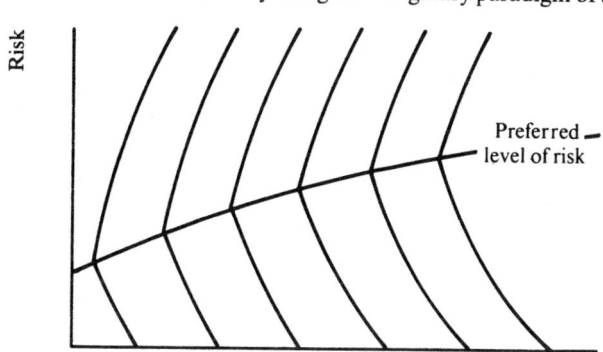

Figure 1. Indifference curves

being tossed into the air. If the coin landed on a specified side you, as the subject, would be given the monetary value of the coin, otherwise you had to pay the experimenter that amount. Perceived riskiness was varied by altering the denomination of the coin and the number of coin tosses you were committed to play. All the coin-tossing gains had the same expected value: zero. Coombs and Meyer found that both gambling for higher denominations and tossing more coins at a time were, on average, considered riskier than tossing smaller denomination coins or fewer coins at a time.

In a further development of his theory Coombs[9] theorized that individuals prefer more risk for less expected value up to an individually determined ideal level of risk. Above this ideal level of risk, increased risk must be compensated for by increased expected value. Figure 1 summarizes Coombs's theory.

All points on a *single* curve represent gambles that a decision-maker would be indifferent between. Gambles represented by points on the curves drawn on the right-hand side, would be preferred to gambles represented by points on the curves to the left-hand side, due to their higher expected value.

Coombs and Huang[10] constructed a sample of the gambles represented by different points on the indifference curves, determined for each individual's preferred level of risk. Subjects' preferences for the gambles supported the theory. It is worth noting that Coombs is not concerned with a definition of 'risk'.

> 'One of the primitives of portfolio theory is the riskiness of a gamble which is left undefined. Any interpretation of the theory for experimental purposes would, of course, require an operational or empirical definition of risk. But it is important to recognize that theory about risk itself is independent of a theory of preference for risk; one can build and test a theory of risk independently of a theory of risk preference.
>
> The purpose of portfolio theory is to provide a basis for making inferences about the riskiness of gambles from preferential choices. The theory is eminently testable and leads to the study of risk with no *a priori* assumptions or semantic confusion about its nature intruding into an experiment' (p. 71).[11]

Alternatively, Payne and Braunstein[12] have presented a 'Contingent Process Model' of choice between paired duplex gambles. This model is essentially a model of the process of the evaluation of a pair of gam-

Descriptive Theories of Decision-making

bles. In the model the decision-maker first evaluates the relative probabilities. If, in each gamble, the probability of winning (PW) is always less than the probability of losing (PL) then the gamble with the lower PL is preferred. However, if PW is greater than PL in each gamble the decision-maker chooses the gamble that has the highest amount to win ($\$W$). If $\$W$ is the same in both gambles then the gamble with the larger PW is chosen. However, if PW is equal to PL in each gamble some subjects choose the gamble with the smaller PL (remember that in duplex gambles the sum of PW and PL does not need to sum to one), while other subjects proceed to evaluate $\$W$. Payne and Braunstein's contingent process model is detailed in the form of a flow chart in Figure 2.

Although this model may seem limited in that its range of applicability is to choice between pairs of duplex gambles, it was one of the first attempts at presenting a process description of decision-making in a detailed sequential way. In many ways it was the forerunner of process-orientated approaches to decision-making, which I will describe in detail in a later section of this chapter.

Yet another descriptive model of decision-making under uncertainty has been developed by Kahneman and Tversky.[13] Their 'Prospect Theory' was developed to account for the observed inconsistencies between behavioural decision-making and SEU. In particular they noted the tendency for people to choose against the sure-thing axiom of SEU in Allais' paradox.[14] Kahneman and Tversky argued that people overweight outcomes that are considered certain, relative to outcomes which are merely probable – a phenomenon which they labelled the 'certainty effect'. Thus people tend to be risk-averse with potential positive payoffs. However, when the payoffs in Allais-type problems are reversed so that gains are replaced by losses, Kahneman and Tversky obtained what they called 'the reflection effect'; for example, the majority of their subjects were willing to accept a risk of a 0·8 chance to lose 4,000 Israeli pounds in preference to a sure loss of 3,000, even though the gamble has a lower expected value (–3,200). To quote Kahneman and Tversky:

> 'In the positive domain, the certainty effect contributes to a risk-averse preference for a sure gain over a larger gain that is merely probable. In the negative domain, the same effect leads to a risk-seeking preference function for a loss that is merely probable over a smaller loss that is certain. The same psychological principle – the

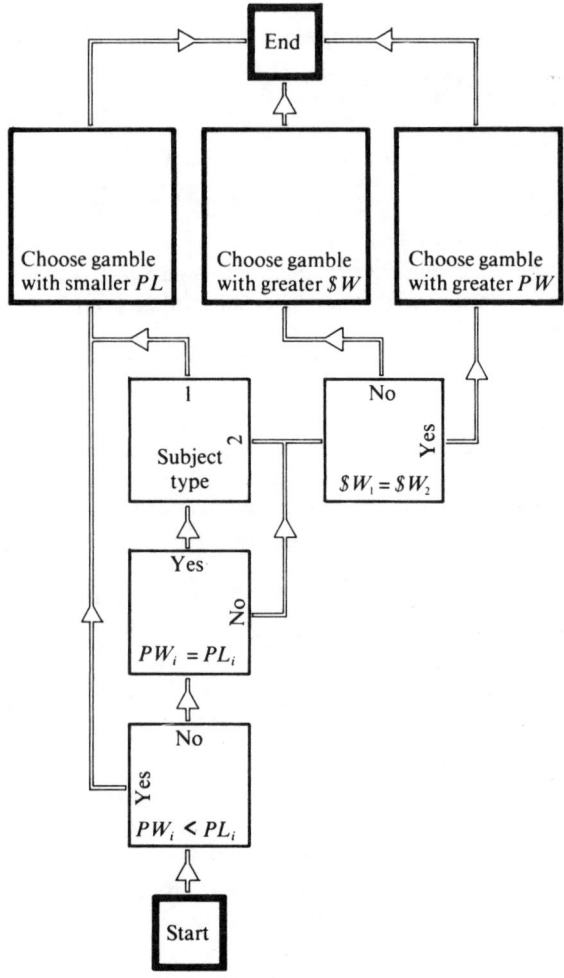

Figure 2. The contingent process model of choice between paired duplex gambles

From J. W. Payne and M. L. Braunstein, 'Preferences among gambles with equal underlying distributions' (see note 12). Copyright © The American Psychological Association, 1971. Adapted by permission of the authors.

Descriptive Theories of Decision-making

overweighting of certainty – favours risk aversion in the domain of gains and risk-seeking in the domain of losses' (pp. 268–9).

The same pattern was confirmed in hypothetical paper and pencil problems involving the number of lives that might be saved by medical treatment and the number of lives that might be lost in an epidemic.

From their discussion of the 'certainty effect' Kahneman and Tversky go on to argue that probabilities should be replaced by decision weights:

> 'Imagine that you can improve your chances of winning a very desirable prize. Would you pay as much to raise your chance from 30 to 40 per cent as you would to raise your chance from 90 per cent to certainty? It is generally agreed that the former offer is less valuable than the latter. It is also agreed that an increase from impossibility to a probability of 10 per cent is more significant than an increase from 30 to 40 per cent. Thus the difference between certainty and possibility and the difference between possibility and impossibility loom larger than comparable differences in the intermediate range of probability' (p. 138).[15]

This relationship between probability and 'decision weight' is shown in Figure 3.

If we accept Kahneman and Tversky's analysis then the utility functions for money shown in Figures 3 and 4 of Chapter 2 are invalid, for they assume that risk aversion and risk are *independent* of the probabilities involved in a decision made under uncertainty.

Additionally, Kahneman and Tversky argue that the subjective valuation of the possible outcomes of a decision depend on your *reference point* or frame of reference. For example:

> 'Framing effects – consumer behaviour may be particularly pronounced in situations that have a single dimension of cost (usually money) and several dimensions of benefit. An elaborate tape deck is a distinct asset in the purchase of a new car. Its cost, however, is naturally treated as a small increment over the price of the car.
>
> The purchase is made easier by judging the value of the tape deck independently and its cost as an increment. Many buyers of homes have similar experiences. Furniture is often bought with little distress at the same time as a house. Purchases that are postponed, perhaps because the desired items were not available, often appear extravagant when contemplated separately: their cost looms larger

Behavioral Decision Theory

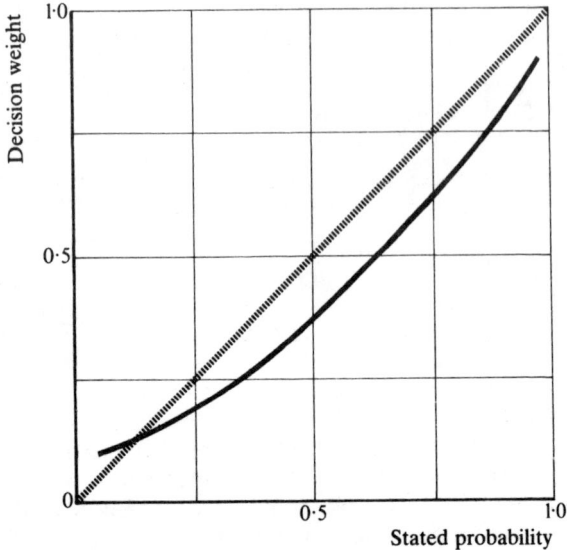

Figure 3. The relationship between probability and decision weight
From D. Kahneman and A. Tversky, 'Prospect theory: An analysis of decision under risk' (see note 13). Adapted by permission of the authors. Copyright © The University of Chicago Press.

on its own. The attractiveness of a course of action may thus change if its cost or benefit is placed in larger account' (p. 140).[16]

Essentially, then, prospect theory's description of decision-making under uncertainty replaces probabilities by decision weights, which need not sum to one, and utility is replaced by a value function, which is determined by an individual's frame of reference. Although Kahneman and Tversky's arguments seem intuitively appealing, it is too soon to say whether prospect theory provides an adequate description of decision-making under uncertainty, in comparison with the other theories we have just discussed.

Choice between Alternatives

From the standpoint of an economist, Herbert Simon has argued that SEU does not describe our decision behaviour but that we make decisions by the principle of 'Satisficing'. Consider the decision problem of selling your house. Offers for purchase are received *sequentially*

Descriptive Theories of Decision-making

and remain active for a limited period of time. If you do not accept an offer within a short period the prospective purchaser may follow up other possibilities. Consider also purchasing a car. Cars are on show in many different showrooms scattered around town, and adverts for private sales appear in the local newspaper every night.

How would you solve these decision problems? Simon would argue that in the first example you would wait until you receive a 'satisfactory' offer. Similarly, in the second example you would continue looking at cars until you spot one that is 'satisfactory' to you. To quote:

> 'In a satisficing model, search terminates when the best offer exceeds an aspiration level that itself adjusts gradually to the value of the offers received so far' (p. 10).[17]

Of course, it would be possible to characterize these sorts of decisions in terms of SEU. On receiving an offer or seeing a car it would be possible to assess the *subjective probability* of receiving a better offer or seeing a better car. Similarly, the *utility attributes* of a delayed sale or the tedium of travelling to other car showrooms could be incorporated to an SEU analysis. However, Simon dismisses this SEU analysis as a description of decision-making:

> 'But utility maximization . . . was not essential . . . for it would have required the decision-maker to be able to estimate the marginal costs and returns of a search in a decision situation that was already too complex for the exercise of global rationality . . . the important thing about search and satisficing theory is that it showed how choice could actually be made with reasonable amounts of calculation, and using very incomplete information, without the need of performing the impossible – of carrying out the optimizing procedure' (p. 503).[18]

Little research has attempted to evaluate the relative effectiveness of satisficing as a description of decision-making. However, the theory and examples are, to my mind, intuitively convincing descriptions of the way decisions are made when alternatives are evaluated sequentially.

Another approach to choice between alternatives has been developed by Amos Tversky.[19] In contrast to Herbert Simon, Tversky deals with simultaneous choice between alternatives rather than to sequential search through alternatives. In his 'Elimination by Aspects' (EBA) theory, Tversky views choice alternatives as multi-attributed. For example, cars can be described in terms of attributes of price, number of seats, speed etc.[20] According to the theory, at each stage in the choice process an attribute or aspect is selected for evaluation with a probability according to its weighting or importance. Choice alternatives that do not include the selected aspect are eliminated from the alternatives under consideration. For example, imagine that you are choosing a new car and that the most important aspect to you is its price. The most you can afford to pay is £4,000. In terms of Tversky's theory all cars with prices above £4,000 will be eliminated from your choice of alternatives. Next, you consider number of seats, your next most important attribute. As you have a family of three growing children, all cars with two seats will be eliminated. Elimination by aspects would then continue until only one car was left uneliminated.

Elimination by aspects is, of course, a contrast to MAUT decomposition introduced in Chapter 2. Recall that a MAUT analysis involves weighting each of the aspects or attributes, scaling each alternative under consideration on each of the attributes and finally computing the MAUT re-composition rule. The alternative with the greatest multi-attributed utility is then chosen. It is easy to see that elimination by aspects and MAUT may specify different choices between alternatives. Consider one example of an attempted manipulation of the tendency to choose by elimination by aspects:

> 'The following television commercial serves to introduce the problem: "There are more than two dozen companies in the San Francisco area which offer training in computer programming." The announcer puts some two dozen eggs and one walnut on the table to represent the alternatives, and continues: "Let us examine the facts. How many of these schools have on-line computer facilities for training?" The announcer removes several eggs. "How many of these schools have placement services that would help find you a job?" The announcer removes some more eggs. "How many of these schools are approved for veterans' benefit?" This continues until the walnut alone remains. The announcer cracks the nutshell, which reveals the name of the company, and concludes: "This is all you need to know in a nutshell" ' (Tversky, op. cit., p. 297).

The above example shows that EBA is easy to apply, involves no complicated numerical computations and is easy to explain and justify to others. However, as Tversky notes:

> 'Its uncritical application, however, may lead to very poor de-

Descriptive Theories of Decision-making

cisions. For virtually any available alternative, no matter how inadequate it may be, we can devise a sequence of selected aspects or, equivalently, describe a particular state of mind that leads to the choice of that alternative . . . From a normative standpoint, the major flaw in the principle of elimination by aspects lies in its failure to ensure that the alternatives retained are, in fact, superior to those which are eliminated' (ibid., p. 298).

Is EBA descriptive of choice behaviour among multi-attributed alternatives? Slovic[21] asked subjects to choose between pairs of alternatives that they had previously equated in value. Within each pair one of the alternatives was scaled higher than the other on a highly weighted attribute, but at the same time was far inferior on a low weighted attribute, such that the two alternatives balanced. Slovic found that when his subjects were *forced* to choose between the paired alternatives the majority chose the alternative which was superior on the highly weighted dimension. Slovic argued that this

'could lead one to reject alternatives whose *overall* utilities (assessed outside the choice context) are superior to those of the chosen alternative' (op. cit. p. 287).

Multi-attributed Inference and Prediction

One of the major data bases used for experimentation on multi-attributed inference has been that collected by Meehl.[22] The judgemental problem used was that of differentiating psychotic from neurotic patients on the basis of their MMPI profiles.

Each patient upon being admitted to hospital had taken the MMPI. Expert clinical psychologists believe (or at least used to believe) that they can differentiate between psychotics and neurotics on the basis of profile of the eleven scores. Meehl noted that

'because the differences between psychotic and neurotic profile are considered in MMPI lore to be highly configural in character, an atomistic treatment by combining scales linearly should be theoretically a very poor substitute for the configural approach'.

Initially researchers tried to 'capture' or 'model' expert judges by a simple linear regression equation. These judgemental representations are constructed in the following fashion. The clinician is asked to make his diagnostic or prognostic judgement from a previously

Behavioral Decision Theory

quantified set of cues for each of a large number of patients. These judgements are then used as the dependent variable in a standard linear regression analysis. The independent variables in this analysis are the values of the cues. The results of such an analysis are a set of

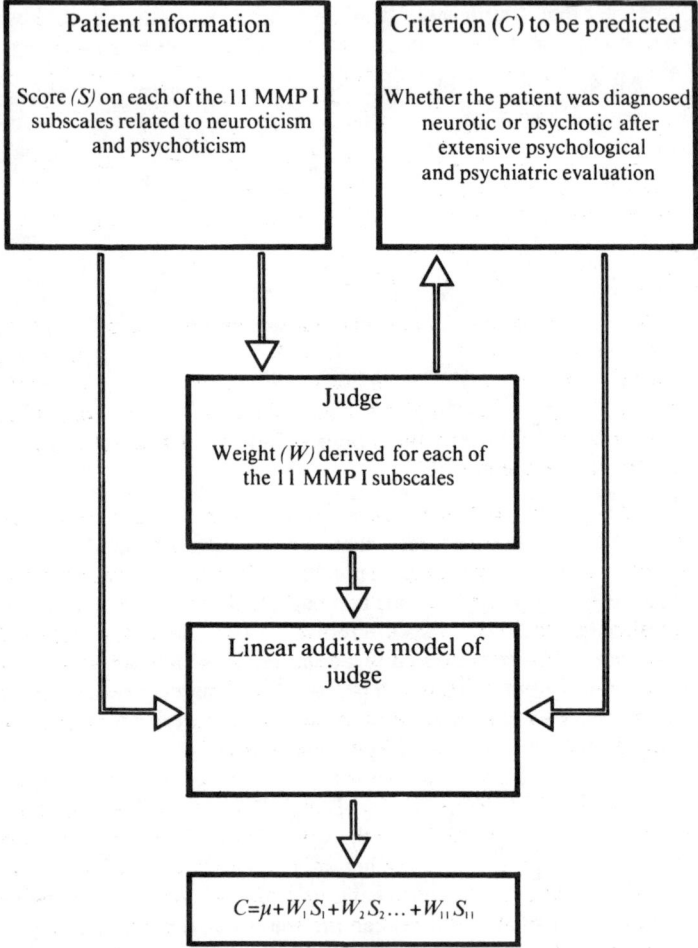

Figure 4. Basic paradigm for the construction of a linear additive model of a judge

Descriptive Theories of Decision-making

regression weights, one for each cue, and these sets of regression weights are referred to as the judge's 'model' or his 'policy'. Figure 4 sets out the basic paradigm for a study of multi-attributed inference.

How do these models make out as predictors themselves? That is, if the regression weights (generated from an analysis of one clinical judge) were used to obtain a 'predicted score' for each patient, would these scores be more valid, or less valid, than the original clinical judgements from which the regression weights were derived? To the extent that the model fails to capture valid non-linear variance to the judges' decision processes, it should perform worse than the judge; to the extent that it eliminates the random error component in human judgements, it should perform better than the judge.

What were the results of this research? The overwhelming conclusion was that the linear model of the judge's behaviour outperformed the judge. Dawes noted:

> 'I know of no studies in which human judges have been able to improve upon optimal statistical prediction . . . A mathematical model by its very nature is an abstraction of the process it models; hence if the decision-maker's behaviour involves following valid principles but following them poorly these valid principles will be abstracted by the model.'[23]

Goldberg[24] reported an intensive study of clinical judgement, pitting experienced and inexperienced clinicians against linear models and a variety of nonlinear or configural models in the psychotic/neurotic prediction task. He was led to conclude that Meehl chose the wrong task for testing the clinicians' purported ability to utilize complex configural relationships. The clinicians achieved a 62 per cent rate, while the simple linear composite achieved 70 per cent. A 50 per cent hit rate could have been achieved by chance as the criterion base rate was approximately 50 per cent neurotic, 50 per cent psychotic.

Dawes and Corrigan[25] have called the replacement of the decision-maker by his model *bootstrapping*. Belief in the efficacy of bootstrapping is based on a comparison of the validity of the linear model of the judge with the validity of his or her holistic judgements. However, as Dawes and Corrigan point out, that is only one of two logically possible comparisons. The other is between the validity of the linear model or the judge and the validity of linear models in general. That is, to demonstrate that bootstrapping works because the linear model catches the essence of a judge's expertise and at the same time eliminates unre-

Behavioral Decision Theory

liability, it is necessary to demonstrate that the weights obtained from an analysis of the judge's behaviour are superior to those that might be obtained in another way – for example, obtained randomly.

Dawes and Corrigan constructed random linear models to predict the criterion. The sign of each predictor variable was determined on an *a priori* basis so that it would have a positive relationship to the critèrion.

On average, correlations between the criterion and the output predicted from the random models were *higher* than those obtained from the judge's models. Dawes and Corrigan also investigated equal weighting and discovered that such weighting was even better than the model of the judges or the random linear models. In all cases equal weighting was superior to the models based on judges' behaviour.

Dawes and Corrigan concluded that the human decision-maker need specify with very little precision the weightings to be used in the decision – at least in the context studied; what must be specified is the variables to be utilized in the linear additive model. It is precisely this knowledge of 'what to look for' in reaching a decision that is the province of the expert clinician. Again, as shown in the previous chapters of this book, it is *not* in the ability to *integrate* information that the decision-maker excels.

The distinction between knowing what to look for and the ability to integrate information is illustrated in a study by Einhorn.[26] Expert doctors coded biopsies of patients with Hodgkin's disease and then made an overall rating of severity. These overall ratings were very poor predictors of survival time, but the *variables* the doctors coded made excellent predictions when utilized in a linear additive model.

In conclusion, we can say that in a multivariate prediction task only the knowledge of which variables to include in the prediction equation is important. Clinical expertise is, of course, the source of this knowledge – without it the linear models could not work. However, the clinician's importance weightings are not at all crucial. This result remains true in all the contexts so far investigated.

Conflict and Decision-making

Janis and Mann provide a different perspective on decision-making from those approaches so far considered in their 'Conflict Theory of Decision-Making':

Descriptive Theories of Decision-making

'Intense conflicts are likely to arise whenever a person has to make an important decision, such as whether to get married, take a new job, sign a business contract . . . Such conflicts become acute as the decision-maker becomes aware of the risk of suffering serious losses from whatever course of action he selects. In addition to these hot cognitions there are others pertaining to difficulties of reversing the decision, which also contribute to the intensity of decisional conflict. Beset with uncertainties, the decision-maker is reluctant to make an irrevocable choice.

When we speak of "decisional conflicts" we are referring to simultaneous opposing tendencies within the individual to accept and reject a given course of action. The most prominent symptoms of such conflicts are hesitation, vacillation, feelings of uncertainty, and signs of acute emotional stress whenever the decision comes within the focus of attention. A major subjective characteristic of decisional conflicts is an unpleasant feeling of distress' (p. 46).[27]

Janis and Mann have identified five main types of decisional behaviour, called 'coping patterns', that are a result of decisional conflict. They argue that whichever coping pattern a person adopts depends on certain conditions. Of the five coping patterns only one, *vigilance*, is likely to result in good decision-making. Janis and Mann's theory is summarized in the flow chart presented in Figure 5.

The flow chart begins if you, as the decision-maker, believe there to be negative feedback about your present course of action, defined to include interaction. If you consider the risks, defined in terms of possible serious losses or lost opportunities, to be inconsequential then you will adhere to your present course of action. However, if you believe that the risks are serious if you do not change your course of action then the question arises as to whether the risks are serious if you do change. If the risks are not serious then you will change your present course of action. However, if the risks are serious if you do change then you are in a situation of decisional conflict, for there are important gains and losses both from keeping to your present course of action and from changing to the first alternative that you just considered. You are therefore confronted with Question 3 and must ask yourself if it is realistic to find another better course of action. If it is not then you will defend your first course of action by avoiding the decision. *Defensive avoidance* can take three forms: *procrastination* involves postponing the decision; *buck-passing* involves shifting the

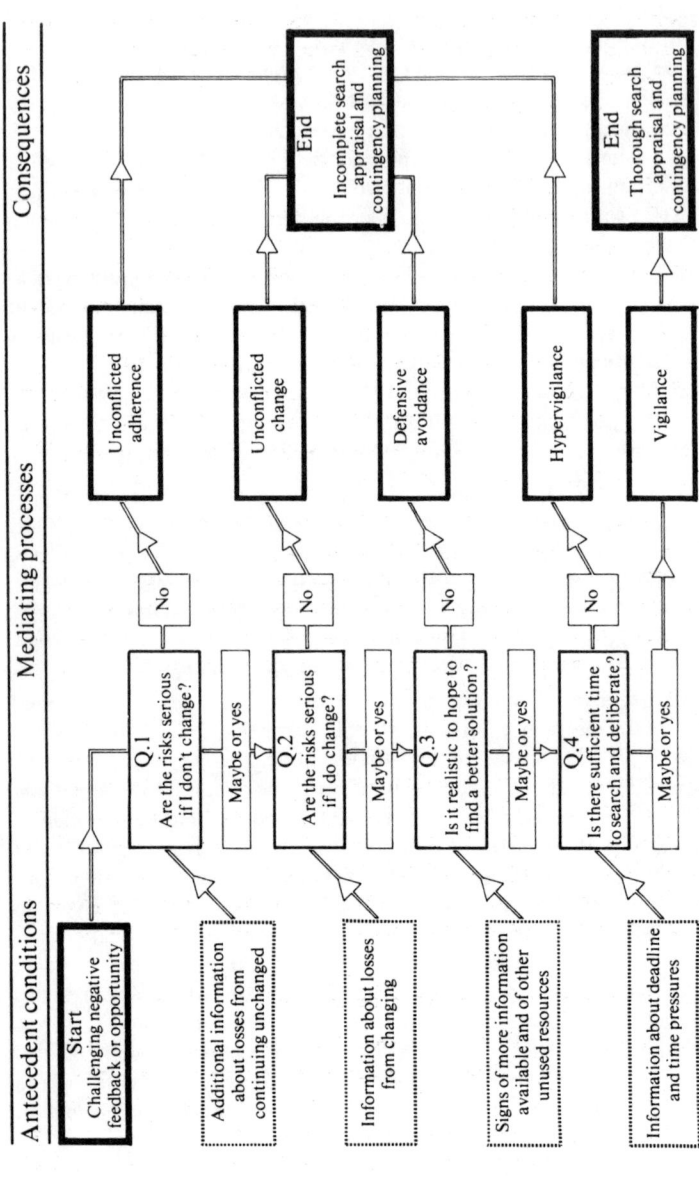

Figure 5. Janis and Mann's conflict theory of decision-making
From I. L. Janis and L. Mann, *Decision-making: A Psychological Analysis of Conflict, Choice and Commitment* (see note 27). Copyright © The Free Press, a Division of Macmillan Publishing Company, 1977. Reprinted by permission of Macmillan

Descriptive Theories of Decision-making

responsibility of the decision to someone else; *bolstering* includes exaggerating the favourable consequences of a course of action and minimizing the unfavourable consequences. Examples of bolstering are given by Janis and Mann:

> 'For example, when offered the honour of heading an important committee that will require an enormous amount of time and energy the nominee may reduce the stress of indecision by overestimating the prestige to be gained . . . the well-known "sour grapes" rationalization. A scientist in an industrial organization may acknowledge that certain good consequences like gaining more money, achieving more prestige, and having more freedom to work in self-selected projects will attend his accepting an offer to become head of a new laboratory, but if he is strongly inclined to reject the opportunity he can discount these attractive considerations by developing rationalizations that enable him to belittle the gains he is renouncing (e.g., by conjuring up the corrupting effects of power)' (op. cit. p. 91).

According to Janis and Mann the type of cognitive defence depends on the predispositions of the decision-maker and the type of decision.

Alternatively, if you feel that it is realistic to find a better solution to your decision problem *but* there is insufficient time available for you to search and deliberate, you will become *hypervigilant* or, in everyday terms, *panic-stricken*. Hypervigilance would seem to be typical of emergency situations.

Only when you are aware of the serious nature of both adhering to and changing from your present course of action, and when you believe there is a better course of action available with the necessary time to search for it and deliberate about it, will your coping pattern be one of *vigilance*. Vigilance involves a thorough consideration of alternative courses of action, an evaluation of costs and risks and a search for relevant information. In many ways this coping pattern can perhaps be seen to be an analogue of unemotional, rational SEU theory.

Current Trends: Process Tracing Techniques

The research presented in Chapters 2, 3 and 5 showed that many decisions and judgements are sub-optimal, relative to normative theories. Decision-makers may be subject to: heuristics and biases in the assessment of probability; overconfidence in probability estimation; probability and variance preferences; and the misperception and misaggregation of probabilistic information in probability revision. However, many of these findings of sub-optimality were, as we saw, essentially pre-theoretical in that the reasons for the sub-optimalities were little developed.

The results and interpretation of this type of research on the shortcomings of human decision-making has been aptly summarized by Paul Slovic.

> 'This work has led to the sobering conclusion that, in the face of uncertainty, man may be an intellectual cripple, whose intuitive judgements and decisions violate many of the fundamental principles of optimal behaviour. These intellectual deficiencies underscore the need for decision-aiding techniques . . .'[28]

Other researchers have adopted a different approach to the analysis of decision-making. Instead of studying final decisions and comparing these to normative models, researchers primarily interested in the development of descriptive theories of choice and decision have attempted to describe the *process* by which final decisions are achieved rather than the output of the process itself. Some of the theories deriving from this approach were described earlier in this chapter. Next I will describe some recent advances in process-tracing techniques.

Recent methods that have become extensively used to gather process-tracing information about decision-making include recording of eye movements and verbal protocols.

Eye-movement data collected by computer controlled systems involving eye-position sensors and recording equipment were used by Russo and Rosen[29] to examine the strategies used in choice between several multi-attributed alternatives. The details of six used cars were displayed in terms of make, year made and mileage. Russo and Rosen examined the sequence of eye fixations with the aim of linking these information acquisition responses to underlying decision strategies. Their data indicated that subjects tended to make comparisons between pairs of alternatives on a single attribute, the EBA approach. Verbal protocols or 'think aloud' reports elicited from their subjects as they made their choices validated the eye-movement data.

Process-tracing techniques have revealed that the more attributes and alternatives there are in a decision problem, the smaller the percentage of these aspects considered. Also the format in which the information is presented strongly affects the search through the information, increasing either intra-alternative or intra-attribute search.[30]

Descriptive Theories of Decision-making

One general conclusion to be drawn from process-tracing studies is that more use should be made of multi-method approaches that will, in theory, produce convergent validation that a particular process is operating. For little is known about the effects of the various process-tracing techniques and their associated requirements for problem presentation on the elicited decision behaviour.

The general strength of verbal protocols is their ability to reveal larger strategies than the micro-analysis of eye-movement data. It may be that requiring subjects to produce verbal protocols whilst they decide may slow down or interrupt the decision processes. To counter this possible criticism Russo[31] has proposed what he calls a 'prompted protocol', where a retrospective protocol is collected while the subject is prompted by a replay of his sequence of eye fixations.

Currently the new technology of process-tracing is under development. Indeed there is, as yet, no agreed-upon procedure for its analysis. As Payne, Braunstein and Carroll note:

> 'While the value of a process tracing approach is evident, it is also clear that definite costs are associated with it. Verbal protocols, for example, provide researchers with large amounts of detailed data, which at present cannot be simply run through a computer program for analysis. Consequently, experiments involving process tracing techniques often require more time and effort than traditional experiments with just input-output analysis . . . standard summary statistics for process data are not well-developed . . . process tracing techniques such as verbal protocols and eye-movement recording are obtrusive measures of behaviour. Opening up the black box usually requires some contact with the box. The limited data available, however, does not indicate that such techniques as verbal protocols alter the decision process in any fundamental way' (p. 41).[32]

Summary

This chapter introduced several descriptive theories of decision-making: Slovic and Lichtenstein's additive linear model, Shanteau's information integration theory, Coombs's portfolio theory of risk, Payne and Braunstein's contingent process model, and Kahneman and Tversky's prospect theory were shown to be alternative descriptions of decision-making under uncertainty. In the context of choice

Behavioral Decision Theory

between alternatives, Simon's theory of satisficing and Tversky's elimination by aspects theory were described.

Research on multi-attributed inference and prediction was outlined and models of the decision-maker were shown to outperform the decision-maker on whom the models were based. The last descriptive decision theory to be considered was Janis and Mann's conflict theory, which views decision-making as a potentially stressful experience.

Finally, recent advances in process-tracing techniques, which show further promise of uncovering the processes by which decisions are made, were evaluated.

Appendices

Appendix 1. Correct answers for the probability assessment questionnaire

1a, 2a, 3b, 4b, 5b, 6b, 7b, 8b, 9b, 10a, 11a, 12a, 13b, 14b, 15b, 16b, 17b, 18b, 19a, 20a, 21b, 22a, 23b, 24a, 25a, 26b, 27b, 28a, 29b, 30a.

Appendix 2. Bayes' theorem posteriors for the draws depicted in Figure 3, from one of the bags shown in Figure 2

	Bag B	Bag Q	Bag W
Draw 1	0·21	0·36	0·43
Draw 2	0·12	0·38	0·50
Draw 3	0·19	0·38	0·43
Draw 4	0·27	0·38	0·35
Draw 5	0·16	0·40	0·44
Draw 6	0·10	0·39	0·51
Draw 7	0·09	0·48	0·43
Draw 8	0·21	0·43	0·36
Draw 9	0·13	0·43	0·44
Draw 10	0·19	0·45	0·36

References

CHAPTER 1

1. My method of introducing subjective expected utility theory is based on an ageing but still excellent introduction given by Edwards, W., Lindman, H., and Phillips, L.D., 'Emerging technologies for making decisions' in Newcomb, T.M. (ed.), *New Directions in Psychology*, vol. II (Holt, Rinehart and Winston, New York, 1965).
2. I have omitted a discussion of the historical development of SEU theory from an economic decision theory to a psychological or subjective decision theory. An early article by Ward Edwards neatly fills this gap: *see* Edwards, W., 'The theory of decision making' in *Psychological Bulletin*, vol. 51 (1954), pp. 380–417.
3. In fact there are slightly different axioms and axiom systems underlying slightly different versions of SEU. These differences need not concern us here, but *see* MacCrimmon, K.R., and Larssen, S., 'Utility theory: Axioms versus "paradoxes"' in *Rational Decisions under Uncertainty*, special volume of Allais, M. (ed.), *Theory and Decisions* (in press).
4. This example of the sure-thing principle is adapted from Edwards, Lindman and Phillips (*see* note 1). I tried to think of a good alternative illustration but found it surprisingly difficult.
5. Christensen-Szalanski, J.J.J., and Bushyhead, J. B., 'Decision analysis as a descriptive model of physician decision-making' in *Technical Report*, vol. 45 (Department of Health Service Research, University of Washington, 1979).
6. Von Winterfeldt, D.V., 'Structuring decision problems for decision analysis' in *Acta Psychologica*, vol. 45 (1980), pp. 71–93.
7. Fischhoff, B., 'Decision analysis – Clinical art or clinical science?' in Sjöberg, L., Tyszka, T., and Wise, J. A. (eds.), *Human Decision Making* (Doxa, Bodafors, in press).
8. Keeney, R., 'Decision analysis in the geo-technical and environmental fields' in Sjöberg, L., Tyszka, T., and Wise, J. A. (eds.), *Human Decision Making* (Doxa, Bodafors, in press).
9. The elicitation technique underlying this program is detailed in Chapter 2.

References

See also Humphreys, P., and Wisudha, A., 'MAUD – an interactive computer program for the structuring, decomposition and recomposition of preferences between multi-attributed alternatives' in *Technical Report*, 79-2 (2nd edition, Decision Analysis Unit, Brunel University, 1980).
10. *See* note 6.
11. Humphreys, P., 'Decision aids: Aiding decisions' in Sjöberg, L., Tyszka, T., and Wise, J.A. (eds.), *Human Decision Making* (Doxa, Bodafors, in press).
12. Fischhoff, B., Slovic, P., and Lichtenstein, S., 'Fault trees: Sensitivity of estimated failure probabilities to problem representation' in *Journal of Experimental Psychology: Human Perception and Performance*, vol. 4 (1978), pp. 330–44.
13. *See* note 7.

CHAPTER 2

1. In this section only methods for the elicitation of point probabilities are considered, since research on the psychology of decision-making has used these point estimates almost exclusively. Methods for the assessment of probability density functions across uncertain quantities are detailed in Seaver, D.A., von Winterfeldt, D., and Edwards, W., 'Eliciting subjective probability distributions on continuous variables' in *Organizational Behavior and Human Performance*, vol. 21 (1978), pp. 379–91.
2. For example, Beach, L.R., and Phillips, L.D., 'Subjective probabilities inferred from estimates and bets' in *Journal of Experimental Psychology*, vol. 75 (1967), pp. 354–9.
3. For example, Winkler, R.L., 'The assessment of prior distributions in Bayesian analysis' in *Journal of the American Statistical Association*, vol. 62 (1967), pp. 776–800.
4. Goodman, B.C., 'Direct estimation procedures for eliciting judgement about uncertain events', in Engineering Psychology Technical Report 011313-5-T (University of Michigan, 1973).
5. Lichtenstein, S., and Newman, J.R., 'Empirical scaling of common verbal phrases associated with numerical probabilities' in *Psychonomic Science*, vol. 9 (1967), pp. 563–4.
6. *See* Markowitz, H., 'The utility of wealth' in *Mathematical Models of Human Behavior* (Dunlop, Stamford, Conn., 1955).
7. This quotation is from Edwards, W., 'Behavioural Decision Theory' in *Annual Review of Psychology* (1961).
8. Humphreys, P.C., and Humphreys, A.R., 'An investigation of subjective preference orderings for multi-attributed alternatives' in Wendt, D., and Vlek, C. (eds.), *Utility, Probability and Human Decision Making* (Reidel, Dordrecht, 1975).
9. Edwards, W., 'Use of multi-attribute utility measurement for social

decision-making' in Bell, D. F., Keeney, R. L., and Raiffa, H. (eds.), *Conflicting Objectives in Decisions* (John Wiley and Sons, Chichester, 1977).
10. I have not introduced multi-attributed utility theory in a formal way, as I did SEU theory, because the various axioms are quite technical. The interested reader is referred to Humphreys, P.C., 'Applications of multi-attribute utility theory' in Jungermann, H., and de Zeeuw, G. (eds.), *Decision Making and Change in Human Affairs* (Reidel, Amsterdam, 1977).
11. Much of their work is reviewed in Tversky, A., and Kahneman, D., 'Judgement under uncertainty: Heuristics and biases' in *Science*, vol. 185 (1974), pp. 1124–31.
12. Lichtenstein, S., Slovic, P., Fischhoff, B., Layman, M., and Coombs, B., 'Judged frequency of lethal events' in *Journal of Experimental Psychology: Human Learning and Memory*, vol. 4 (1978), pp. 551–78.
13. Slovic, P., 'From Shakespeare to Simon: Speculations – and some evidence – about man's ability to process information' in Research Monograph, vol. 12, no. 12 (Oregon Research Institute, April 1972).
14. Dostoevsky, F., *The Gambler*, translated by MacAndrew, A.R. (Bantam Books, New York, 1964).
15. Kahneman, D., and Tversky, A., 'Intuitive prediction: Biases and corrective procedures' in Makridakis, S., and Wheelwright, S.C. (eds.), *TIMS Studies: Management Science*, vol. 20 (1977), pp. 313–27.
16. Lichtenstein, S., and Fischhoff, B., 'Do those who know more also know more about how much they know?' in *Organizational Behavior and Human Performance*, vol. 20 (1977), pp. 159–83.
17. Koriat, A., Lichtenstein, S., and Fischhoff, B., 'Reasons for confidence' in *Journal of Experimental Psychology: Human Learning and Memory*, vol. 6 (1980), pp. 107–18.
18. Fischhoff, B., and Beyeth, R., '"I knew it would happen": Remembered probabilities of once-future things' in *Organizational Behavior and Human Performance*, vol. 13 (1975), pp. 1–16.

CHAPTER 3

1. Edwards, W., 'The prediction of decisions among bets' in *Journal of Experimental Psychology*, vol. 50 (1955), pp. 201–14.
2. I have equated expected value (EV), which involves multiplying the stated probability by the payoff, with SEU, which is the product of the subjective probability and the subjective value, or utility, of the payoff.
3. Lichtenstein, S., Slovic, P., and Zink, D., 'Effect of instruction in expected value on optimality of gambling decisions' in *Journal of Experimental Psychology*, vol. 79 (1969), pp. 236–40.
4. Lichtenstein, S., and Slovic, P., 'Reversals of preference between bids and choices in gambling decisions' in *Journal of Experimental Psychology*, vol. 89 (1971), pp. 46–55.

References

5. Slovic, P., 'From Shakespeare to Simon: Speculations – and some evidence – about man's ability to process information' in Research Monograph, vol. 12, no. 12 (Oregon Research Institute, April 1972).
6. Tversky, A., 'Intransitivity of preferences' in *Psychological Review*, vol. 79 (1969), pp. 281–99.
7. Coombs, C.H., and Pruitt, D.G., 'Components of risk in decision making: Probability and variance preferences' in *Journal of Experimental Psychology*, vol. 60 (1960), pp. 265–77.
8. Lichtenstein, S., 'Bases for preferences among three-outcome bets' in *Journal of Experimental Psychology*, vol. 69 (1965), pp. 162–9.
9. Rapoport, A., and Wallsten, T.S., 'Individual decision behaviour' in *Annual Review of Psychology*, vol. 23 (1972), pp. 131–76 – well worth reading.
10. Slovic, P., and Lichtenstein, S., 'Importance of variance preferences in gambling decisions' in *Journal of Experimental Psychology*, vol. 78 (1968), pp. 646–54.
11. Payne, J.W., and Braunstein, M.L., 'Preferences among gambles with equal underlying distributions' in *Journal of Experimental Psychology*, vol. 87 (1971), pp. 13–18.
12. Ellsberg, D., 'Risk, ambiguity and the Savage axiom' in *Quarterly Journal of Economics* (1961), pp. 670–89.
13. Allais, M., 'Le comportement de l'homme rationnel devant le risque: Critique des postulats et axiomes de l'école américaine' in *Econometrica*, vol. 21 (1953), pp. 503–46.
14. MacCrimmon, K., 'Descriptive and normative implications of the decision-theory postulates' in Borch, C., and Mossiv, J. (eds.), *Risk and Uncertainty* (Macmillan, New York, 1968).
15. Slovic, P., and Tversky, A., 'Who accepts Savage's axiom?' in *Behavioral Science*, vol. 19 (1974), pp. 368–73.

CHAPTER 4

1. Specifically,

$$H = -\sum_{i=1}^{i=M} \frac{n_i}{N} \log_2 \frac{n_i}{N}$$

where n_i is the number of assessments of a given probability, M is the number of different probability assessments made by the individual and $N = \Sigma_i = 75$.

2. Souief, M.I., 'Extreme response sets as measures of intolerance of ambiguity' in *British Journal of Psychology*, vol. 49 (1958), pp. 329–33.
3. Bochner, S., 'Defining intolerance of ambiguity' in *Psychological Record*, vol. 15 (1965), pp. 393–400.

4. Budner, S., 'Intolerance of ambiguity as a personality variable' in *Journal of Personality*, vol. 30 (1962), pp. 29–50.
5. Adorno, T.C., Fenkel-Brunswik, E., Levinson, P.J., and Sanford, R.N., *The Authoritarian Personality* (Norton, New York, 1960), p. 480.
6. Rokeach, M., *The Open and Closed Mind* (Basic Books, New York, 1960), p. 56.
7. Ertel, S., 'Erkenntnis und Dogmatismus' in *Psychologische Rundschau*, vol. 23 (1972), pp. 241–69.
8. Wright, G.N., and Phillips, L.D., 'Personality and probabilistic thinking: An exploratory study' in *British Journal of Psychology*, vol. 70 (1979), pp. 295–303.
9. For example, *see* Kohn, P.M., 'Authoritarianism, rebelliousness and their correlates among British undergraduates' in *British Journal of Social and Clinical Psychology*, vol. 13 (1974), pp. 245–55.
10. For a summary, *see* Wright, G.N., and Phillips, L.D., 'Decision making – cognitive style or task specific behaviour?' in Bonarius, H., van Heck, G., and Smid, N. (eds.), *Personality Psychology in Europe* (Lawrence Erlbaum Associates, in press).
11. Alker, H.A., 'Relevance of person perception to clinical psychology' in *Journal of Consulting and Clinical Psychology*, vol. 37 (1971), pp. 167–76.
12. Mischel, W., 'On the empirical dilemmas of psychodynamic approaches: Issues and alternatives' in *Journal of Abnormal Psychology*, vol. 28 (1973), pp. 334–5.
13. Endler, N.S., 'The case for person–situation interactions' in *Canadian Psychological Review*, vol. 16 (1975), pp. 319–29.
14. Ekehammar, B., 'Interactionism in personality from a historical perspective' in *Psychological Bulletin*, vol. 81 (1974), pp. 1026–48.
15. Peterson, C.R., and Beach, L.R., 'Man as an intuitive statistician' in *Psychological Bulletin*, vol. 68 (1967), pp. 29–46.
16. Phillips, L.D., and Edwards, W., 'Conservatism in a simple probability inference task' in *Journal of Experimental Psychology*, vol. 72 (1966), pp. 346–54.
17. Bayes' theorem is discussed in detail in Chapter 5, p. 82.
18. These two papers present excellent, easily read reviews of the early literature on probability assessment:
    Slovic, P., 'From Shakespeare to Simon: Speculations – and some evidence – about man's ability to process information' in Research Monograph, vol. 12, no. 12 (Oregon Research Institute, April 1972).
    Hogarth, R.M., 'Cognitive processes and the assessment of subjective probability distributions' in *Journal of the American Statistical Association*, vol. 70 (1975), pp. 271–94.
19. Simon, H.A., *Models of Man: Social and National* (Wiley, New York, 1957).
20. By choosing the 'certainty' options in Ellsberg's test of the sure-thing prin-

ciple presented in Chapter 3, Figure 11 (p. 61), i.e. by choosing act 1 in situation A and act 4 in situation B.
21. The topic of probability revision is discussed in Chapter 5.
22. Former undergraduates at Brunel.
23. Mathematical representations of these curves were also computed for each individual. These calibration measures are described in detail in: Wright, G.N., Phillips, L.D., Whalley, P.C., Choo, G.T.G., Ng, K.O., Tan, I., and Wisudha, A., 'Cultural differences in probabilistic thinking' in *Journal of Cross-Cultural Psychology*, vol. 9 (1978), pp. 285–99.
24. Wright, G.N., and Phillips, L.D., 'Cultural variation in probabilistic thinking: Alternative ways of dealing with uncertainty' in *International Journal of Psychology*, vol. 15 (1980), pp. 239–57.
25. Redding, S.G., and Martyn-Johns, T.A., 'Paradigm of differences and their relation to management functions, with reference to South-East Asia' in Centre of Asian Studies Working Paper (University of Hong Kong, 1978).
26. Penny, D.M., 'Development opportunities in Indonesian agriculture' in *Bulletin of Indonesian Economic Studies*, vol. 8 (1967), pp. 35–64.
27. Redding, S.G., 'Bridging the culture gap' in *Asian Business and Investment*, vol. 4 (1978), pp. 45–52.
28. Watson, S.R., and Brown, R.V., 'Case studies in the value of decision analysis' in *Technical Report*, vol. 10 (Decisions and Designs Inc., Maclean, Va., 1975).
29. Humphreys, P.C., 'Decision aids: Aiding decisions' in Sjöberg, L., Tyszka, T., and Wise, J. A. (eds.), *Human Decision Making* (Doxa, Bodafors, in press).
30. A pseudonym!
31. Another pseudonym.
32. Fischhoff, B., 'Decision analysis – Clinical art or clinical science?' in Sjöberg, L., Tyszka, T., and Wise, J. A. (eds.), *Human Decision Making* (Doxa, Bodafors, in press).

CHAPTER 5

1. 'Book-bag' is a term that you will come across constantly in research on Bayes' theorem and so I will use it here. It is an American expression for a college student's bag that is said to contain college books!
2. But recall that this axiom is also a *consequence* of acceptance of the axioms of SEU.
3. Phillips, L.D., Hayes, W.L., and Edwards, W., 'Conservatism in complex probabilistic inference' in *IEEE Transactions in Human Factors in Electronics*, vol. 7 (1966), pp. 7–18.
4. Marks, D.F., and Clarkson, J.K., 'An explanation of conservatism in the book-bag-and-poker-chips situation' in *Acta Psychologica*, vol. 36 (1972), pp. 145–60.

5. Alberoni, F., 'Contribution to the study of subjective probability' in *Journal of General Psychology*, vol. 66 (1962), pp. 241–64.
6. Barclay, S., and Beach, L.R., 'Combinational properties of personal probabilities' in *Organizational Behavior and Human Performance*, vol. 8 (1972), pp. 176–83.
7. Peterson, C.R., Schneider, R.J., and Miller, A.J., 'Sample size and the revision of subjective probability' in *Journal of Experimental Psychology*, vol. 69 (1965), pp. 522–7.
8. *See* note 6.
9. *See* note 7.
10. Pitz, G.F., Downing, L., and Reinhold, H., 'Sequential effects in the revision of subjective probabilities' in *Canadian Journal of Psychology*, vol. 21 (1967), pp. 381–93.
11. DuCharme, W.M., and Peterson, C.R., 'Intuitive inference about normally distributed populations' in *Journal of Experimental Psychology*, vol. 78 (1968), pp. 269–75.
12. Winkler, R.L., and Murphy, A.M., 'Experiments in the laboratory and the real world' in *Organizational Behavior and Human Performance*, vol. 10 (1973), pp. 252–70.
13. When reliability is taken into account the resulting modification of Bayes' theorem is called 'cascaded inference': *see* Schum, D.A., and Pfeiffer, P., 'Observer reliability and human inference' in *IEEE Transactions in Reliability*, R-22 (1973), pp. 170–76.
14. Youssef, Z.I., and Peterson, C.R., 'Intuitive cascaded inferences' in *Organizational Behavior and Human Performance*, vol. 10 (1973), pp. 349–58.
15. Edwards, W., Phillips, L.D., Hayes, W.L., and Goodman, B.C., 'Probabilistic information processing systems: Design and evaluation' in *IEEE Transactions on System Science and Cybernetics*, SSC-4 (1968), pp. 248–65.
16. Kaplan, R.J., and Newman, J.R., 'Studies in probabilistic information processing' in *IEEE Transactions in Human Factors in Electronics*, HFE-7 (1966), pp. 49–63.
17. Domas, P.A., and Peterson, C.R., 'Probabilistic information processing systems: Evaluation with conditionally dependent data' in *Organizational Behavior and Human Performance*, vol. 7 (1960), pp. 77–85.
18. Graham, R.K., and Kendall, B.S., 'Memory-for-Designs Test: revised general manual' in *Perceptual and Motor Skills*, vol. 11 (1960), pp. 147–55.
19. For similar numerical examples and for a more formal introduction to the various forms of Bayes' theorem and their use in statistical inference, *see* Phillips, L.D., *Bayesian Statistics for Social Scientists* (Nelson, London, 1973).
20. Diamond, G.A., and Forrester, J.S., 'Diagnosis of coronary heart disease' in *New England Journal of Medicine*, vol. 300 (1979), pp. 1350–65.
21. For an extensive review, *see* Beech, B.H., 'Expert judgement about uncer-

References

tainty' in *Organizational Behavior and Human Performance*, vol. 14 (1975), pp. 10–51.

CHAPTER 6

1. Slovic, P., and Lichtenstein, S., 'Relative importance of probabilities and payoffs in risk-taking' in *Journal of Experimental Psychology*, vol. 78 (1968), pp. 1–18.
2. *See* Chapter 3 for more details of the procedures used.
3. Shanteau, J.C., 'Component processes in risky decision judgements' (unpublished Doctoral Dissertation, University of California at San Diego, 1970) cited in Shanteau, J.C., 'An information integration analysis of risky decision-making' in Kaplan, M.F., and Schwartz, S. (eds.), *Human Judgement and Decision Processes* (Academic Press, New York, 1975).
4. For a clear exposition, *see* Shanteau, J.C., 'An information integration analysis of risky decision-making' in Kaplan, M.F., and Schwartz, S. (eds.), *Human Judgement and Decision Processes* (Academic Press, New York, 1975).
5. *See* note 4.
6. Anderson, N.H., and Shanteau, J.C., 'Information integration in risky decision-making' in *Journal of Experimental Psychology*, vol. 100 (1970), pp. 29–38.
7. *See* note 4.
8. Coombs, C.H., and Meyer, D.E., 'Risk-preference in coin-toss games' in *Journal of Mathematical Psychology*, vol. 6 (1969), pp. 514–27.
9. Coombs, C.H., 'Portfolio theory and the measurement of risk' in Kaplan, M.F., and Schwartz, S. (eds.), *Human Judgement and Decision Processes* (Academic Press, New York, 1975).
10. Coombs, C.H., and Huang, L.C., 'Tests of portfolio theory of risk preference' in *Journal of Experimental Psychology*, vol. 85 (1970), pp. 23–9.
11. *See* note 9.
12. Payne, J.W., and Braunstein, M.L., 'Preferences among gambles with equal underlying distributions' in *Journal of Experimental Psychology*, vol. 87 (1971), pp. 13–18.
13. Kahneman, D., and Tversky, A., 'Prospect theory: An analysis of decision under risk' in *Econometrica*, vol. 47 (1979), pp. 263–91.
14. *See* Chapter 3 (pp. 51–66) for a full account of research on the acceptability of the axioms of SEU.
15. Kahneman, D., and Tversky, A., 'The psychology of preferences' in *Scientific American* (1982), pp. 136–42.
16. *See* note 15.
17. Simon, H.A., 'Rationality as process and product of thought' in *American*

Economic Association, vol. 68 (1978), pp. 1–16.
18. Simon, H.A., 'Rational decision-making in business organizations' in *The American Economic Review*, vol. 69 (1979), pp. 493–513.
19. Tversky, A., 'Elimination by aspects: A theory of choice' in *Psychological Review*, vol. 79 (1972), pp. 281–99.
20. As we saw in Chapter 2.
21. Slovic, P., 'Choice between equally valued alternatives' in *Journal of Experimental Psychology: Human Perception and Performance*, vol. 1 (1975), pp. 280–87.
22. Meehl, P.E., 'A comparison of clinicians with five statistical methods of identifying psychotic MMPI profiles' in *Journal of Counselling Psychology*, vol. 6 (1959), pp. 102–22.
23. Dawes, R.M., 'Graduate admission variables and future success' in *Science*, vol. 187 (1975), pp. 721–43.
24. Goldberg, L.R., 'Diagnosticians versus diagnostic signs: The diagnosis of psychosis versus neurosis from the MMPI' in *Psychological Monographs*, vol. 79 (1965), pp. 602–43.
25. Dawes, R.M., and Corrigan, B., 'Linear models in decision-making' in *Psychological Bulletin*, vol. 81 (1974), pp. 95–106.
26. Einhorn, H.J., 'Expert measurement and mechanical combination' in *Organizational Behavior and Human Performance*, vol. 7 (1972), pp. 86–106.
27. Janis, I.L., and Mann, L., *Decision-making: A Psychological Analysis of Conflict, Choice and Commitment* (Free Press, New York, 1979).
28. Slovic, P., 'Towards understanding and improving decisions' in Fleishman, E.A. (ed.), *Human Performance and Productivity* (in press).
29. Russo, J.E., and Rosen, L.D., 'An eye fixation analysis of multi-alternative choice' in *Memory and Cognition*, vol. 3 (1975), pp. 267–76.
30. Svenson, O., 'Process descriptions of decision-making' in *Organizational Behavior and Human Performance*, vol. 23 (1979), pp. 86–112.
31. Russo, J.E., 'Eye fixations can save the world: A critical evaluation and comparison between eye fixations and other information processing methodologies' in Hunt, H.K. (ed.), *Advances in Consumer Research* (Ann Arbor, Ann Arbor Association for Consumer Research, 1978).
32. Payne, J.W., Braunstein, M.L., and Carroll, J.S., 'Exploring predecisional behavior: An alternative approach to decision research' in *Organizational Behavior and Human Performance*, vol. 22 (1978), pp. 17–44.

Index

additive model, 97-8
Alberoni, F., 88
Alker, H.A., 71
Allais, M., 62, 63, 64, 101
ambiguity, intolerance of, 68-74
anchoring and adjusting, 42
Anderson, N.H., 99
authoritarianism, 68-74
availability, probability assessment, 41

Barclay, S., 88
Bayes' theorem, 39, 72, 73, 82-95
Beach, L.R., 72, 88
Beyeth, R., 50
biases, probability assessment, 40-44
bidding procedures, 52
Bochner, S., 68
bolstering, 113
bootstrapping, 109
Braunstein, M.L., 58-9, 100, 115
Brown, R.V., 78
Budner, S., 68
Bushyhead, J.B., 18, 19

calibration, 44-50, 71, 77
Carroll, J.S., 115
China, business management, 78
Christensen-Szalanski, J.J.J., 18, 19
Clarkson, J.K., 88
computer aids, 23-4
conflict theory, 110-13
conservatism, opinion revision, 89-91
 probabilistic thinking, 68-74
contingency decisions, 24
contingent process model, 100-101
Coombs, C.H., 55-6, 99-100
coping patterns, 111

Corrigan, B., 109-10
cultural comparisons, probabilistic
 thinking, 74-9

data, and revision of opinion, 89-91, 92
Dawes, R.M., 109-10
decidability, 15
decision analysis, 17-19, 20-21, 25, 40
decision tree, 18-19, 23,24
decision weights, 103-4, 110
decisional conflicts, 111
defensive avoidance, 111, 112
Diamond, G.A., 95
disaster planning, 24
dogmatism, 68-74
Domas, P.A., 92
dominance, 16
Dostoevsky, F., 42-3
Downing, L., 89
DuCharme, W.M., 89-90
duplex gamble, 57-61

Edwards, W., 37, 38, 51, 52, 72, 91-2
Ekehammar, B., 72
elimination by aspects (EBA) theory,
 105-7
Ellsberg, D., 61-2, 64
Endler, N.S., 72
environmental standard setting, 24
Ertel, S., 68
eye-movement data, 114, 115

failure probabilities, 25-7
fault trees, 25
Fischhoff, B., 23, 25-7, 40-49, 50, 79
Forrester, J.S., 95
framing effects, 103

Frenkel-Brunswik, E., 68
frequency of events, probability and, 41

Galton, 43
gamblers' fallacy, 42–3
gambles, additive model, 97–8
  anchoring in subjective valuation of, 42
  choice between single, 51–7
  contingent process model, 100–101
  duplex, 57–61, 100
  information integration theory, 97–8
  portfolio theory of risk, 99–100
  prospect theory, 101–4
Goldberg, L.R., 109
Goodman, B.C., 32, 91
Graham, R.K., 93

Hayes, W.L., 91
heuristic principles, probability assessment, 40–44
Hogarth, R.M., 72
Hong Kong, probabilistic thinking, 74–7
Huang, L.C., 100
Humphreys, A.R., 38
Humphreys, P.C., 24, 25, 38, 78, 79
hypervigilance, 113

Indonesia, probabilistic thinking, 74–7
information integration theory, 98–9, 110
integration, 98–9, 110
intelligence, effect on calibration, 49–50
interactionism, 71–2
intolerance of ambiguity, 68–74
intuitive decisions, 15, 17
intuitive preference ordering, 39–40
intuitive revision of opinion, 82

Janis, I.L., 110–13

Kahneman, D., 40–44, 72, 73, 101–4
Kaplan, R.J., 92
Keeney, R., 23
Kelly, 24
Kendall, B.S., 93
Koriat, A., 50

Lichtenstein, S., 25–7, 32, 41, 48–9, 52, 53, 56, 57, 58, 61, 97–8

MacCrimmon, K., 64–5
Malaysia, probabilistic thinking, 74–7
Mann, L., 110–13
Markowitz, H., 36
Marks, D.F., 88
Martyn-Jones, T.A., 76
mathematical models, 109
MAUD, 24
Maximax strategy, 12–13
Maximin strategy, 13
Meehl, P.E., 107, 109
Memory-for-Designs Test, 93
Meyer, D.E., 99–100
Mischel, W., 71
money, utility function for, 33–8
multi-attributed inference, 107–10
multi-attributed utility theory (MAUT), 38–40, 106
Murphy, A.M., 90–91

Newman, J.R., 92
Ng, F., 74
non-probabilistic thinking, 71, 73, 76–8

objective probabilities, 13
opinion revision, 81–96
OPINT, 24
overconfidence, probability assessment, 48–50

Payne, J.W., 58–9, 100, 115
payoff matrix, 11–12
Penny, D.M., 76
personologism, 71
Peterson, C.R., 72, 88, 89–90, 91, 92
Phillips, L.D., 67, 69, 72, 88, 91
Pitz, G.F., 89
portfolio theory of risk, 99–100
posterior opinion, 81–96, 117
prior opinions, revision of, 81–96
Probabilistic Information Processing Systems (PIP Systems), 91–3
probability, expressions of, 32
  measuring, 29–32
  numerical, 14
  objective, 13
  recalled, 50
  revision of opinion, 81–96
  subjective, 13

Index

probability assessment, anchoring and
  adjusting, 42
 availability and, 41
 biases in assessment, 40–44
 calibration, 44–50
 cultural comparisons, 74–9
 gamblers' fallacy, 42–3
 heuristics of assessment, 40–44
 individual comparisons, 68–74
 misperception of regression towards the
   mean, 43
 opinion reversion, 91–3
 realism of, 44–50
 representativeness and, 41
Probability Assessment Questionnaire
  (PAQ), 67–8
probability preferences, 52
probability reversion, 88, 89
process-tracing studies, 114–15
prospect theory, 101–4
prototypical decision analytic structure, 24
Pruitt, D.G., 55–6

Raiffa, H., 17, 40
Redding, S.G., 76, 78
reflection effect, 101
regression towards the mean, 43–4
Reinhold, H., 89
representativeness, probabilistic
  judgement and, 41
revision of opinion, 81–96
risks, conflict theory, 111
 decisions under uncertainty, 99–100, 103
 in gambles, 99–100
 in SEU, 99
Rokeach, M., 68
Rosen, L.D., 114
Russo, J.E., 114, 115

satisficing model, 104–5
Schlaifer, R., 17
Shanteau, J.C., 98–9
Simon, H.A., 73, 104–5
situationism, 71
Slovic, P., 25–7, 42, 52, 53, 57, 58, 61, 64–65, 72, 88, 97–8, 107, 114
Souief, M.I., 68
subjective expected utility theory (SEU),
  11–28

acceptability of the axioms of, 61–5
 as a normative theory, 15–25
 and complex gambles, 57–61
 decidability, 15
 dominance, 16
 and simple gambles, 51–7, 64
 sure-thing principle, 16
 transitivity, 16
 under uncertainty, 67–80
subjective probabilities, 13, 14
 assessment, 29–32
 revision of opinion, 81–96
subjective values, meaning, 33–40
sure-thing principle, 16, 61–5
symmetry arguments, 63

Tan, I., 74
training, effect on calibration, 49–50
transitivity, 16
Tversky, A., 40–44, 53–4, 64–5, 72, 73, 88, 101–4, 105–7

uncertainty, additive model, 97–8
 contingent process model, 100–101
 cultural comparisons under, 74–9
 decision-making under, 97–104
 individual differences under, 68–74
 information-integration theory, 98–9
 portfolio theory, 99–100
 prospect theory, 101–4
 SEU under, 67–80
utiles, definition, 35
utility, measuring, 33–40
 for money, 33–8
 multi-attributed, 38–40

verbal protocols, 114, 115
View of Uncertainty Questionnaire
  (VUQ), 68
vigilance, 111–13
Von Winterfeldt, D.V., 23, 24

Watson, S.R., 78
Winkler, R.L., 90–91
Wisudha, A., 24, 74

Youssef, Z.I., 91

Zinc, D., 52